ON REFLECTION SERIES

Love your Crooked Neighbour

THOUGIITS ON BREATH, BREAD, BREASTS AND BROKENNESS

RON FERGUSON

Serics Editor.
Duncan B Forrester

D0755667

SAINT ANDREW PRESS
EDINBURGH

First published in 1999 by
SAINT ANDREW PRESS
121 George Street, Edinburgh EH2 4YN

Copyright © Ron Ferguson 1999

ISBN 0 7152 0766 0

British Library Cataloguing in Publication Data
A catalogue record for this book
is available from the British Library.

ISBN 0715207660

Cover design concept by Mark Blackadder.
Printed and bound by Bell and Bain Ltd., Glasgow.

Contents

✳

CONTENTS

Series Editor's Introduction

✶

ALL down the ages Christians have reflected on their faith and its bearing on life. These reflections have taken a great variety of forms, but one of the most common has been the sermon. For generations notable preachers were well-known public figures, and books of sermons were a well-known literary genre. In many places people queued to hear great preachers, whose sermons were reported in the press, and discussed and dissected afterwards. Sermons launched great movements of mission, and revival, and social change. Sometimes influential preachers were imprisoned by the authorities so that their disturbing challenge should not be heard.

Nowhere was this tradition more lively than in Scotland. But today, some people say, the glory has departed. If you want to find great preaching today, the critics say, go to Africa, or Latin America, or to Black churches in the States. No longer in Scotland do people pack in their hundreds into huge churches to hear great preachers. The sermon seems to have lost its centrality in Scottish life. The conviction and the emotional surcharge that once sustained a great succession of notable preachers seems hard to find today. Has secularisation destroyed the appetite for sermons? Has the modern questioning of authority eroded the preaching office? Do Christians no longer reflect on their faith, or do they do it in other and newer ways?

This series of books shows that the tradition of preaching is still very much alive and well. It has changed, it is true, and it has adapted to new circumstances and new challenges. It is not the same as it was in the long afterglow of the Victorian pulpit. Reflection by the Scots on their faith, as these books illustrate, is perhaps more varied than it was in the past, and their sermons are briefer. But Scottish preaching is still passionate, thoughtful, biblical, challenging, and deeply concerned with the relevance of the gospel to the needs of today's world.

The reflections on the Christian faith in these books are challenging, disturbing, nourishing. They proclaim a Word that is alive and active, and penetrates to the depths of things, a Word that speaks of hope and worth, of forgiveness and new beginnings, of justice, peace and love. And so they invite the reader to engage afresh with the everlasting gospel.

Duncan B Forrester
EDINBURGH

ON REFLECTION ...

Other titles available in this series

Wrestle and Fight and Pray
John L Bell

Laughter and Tears
James A Whyte

Go by the Book
Robert Davidson

Acknowledgments

*

THANKS are due to *The Herald* newspaper for permission to use several articles, and to reproduce the photograph of George MacLeod by Angela Catlin. The author would like to acknowledge the co-operation of BBC Radio Scotland. Thanks are also due to Bellew Publishing, London for permission to reproduce the George MacLeod memorial sermon from the book *St Andrews Rock*; to Fountain Publishing for permission to quote from *The Greatest Gift* by Angus Peter Campbell; to Michael Grieve and Routledge & Kegan Paul Ltd for permission to reproduce Hugh MacDiarmid's poem 'The Bonnie Broukit Bairn' in Michael Grieve and Alexander Scott (eds): *The Hugh MacDiarmid Anthology: Poems in Scots and English;* to Wild Goose Publications for permission to use the extract by George MacLeod from *The Whole Earth shall cry glory*; and to Saint Andrew Press for permission to quote from *A Glasgow Bible* by Jamie Stuart

Quotations in this book are taken from the REVISED STANDARD VERSION (RSV), copyright 1946, 1952, © 1971, by the Division of Christian Education of the National Council of the Churches of Christ in the USA, and are used by permission.

Foreword

✳

SOME years ago, I attended a service in East Harlem. It was held in Antioch Baptist Church on New York's 125th Street.

The atmosphere was electric. The singing of the black gospel choir was inspiring, and the congregation joined in joyfully, creating new harmonies and swaying to the rhythm of the music.

Then, the sermon. As the preacher warmed to his theme, the congregation shouted 'Amen', 'Right on!', 'Say it brother!' Encouraged, the minister responded with enthusiasm, the words pouring out of him. Thus the sermon became a joint effort, a happening. The Word became Event, right there in the midst. Then the choir burst into exuberant, multi-coloured singing and clapping.

I realised I wasn't in Scotland.

We're cannier here, more sparing of our emotions. Something to do with the weather? It's hard to hang loose when you're wearing three duffel coats. Or is it the Calvinistic tradition? The hard pews?

At its best, a sermon is a shared event, a happening between pulpit and pew, between a Presbyterian rock and a hard place. And sermons are essentially oral events. They are not intended to be literature.

Written sermons, then, lack a certain something. The context, atmosphere and response are missing. Maybe the reader needs to compensate by vocalising the sermons for the benefit of a kitchen congregation of a dog or cat, and throw in the odd 'Hallelujah!' or 'Rubbish!' Preaching engages the emotions of the preacher, and of the congregation. The preacher also needs to be able to respond to the response, and sometimes even to leave the prepared text or notes behind.

Preaching is not something one ever 'masters'. I am reminded of the perceptive words of the great Archie Craig: 'The paradox of the pulpit is that its occupant is a sinner whose chief right to be there is his perpetual sense that he has no right to be there.'

All preaching is contextual; consequently I have retained the references to the particular historical contexts of the sermons. I have taken the liberty of including a poem, a parable in the form of a short story, reflections for BBC Scotland, and articles written for *The Herald* newspaper, on the grounds that there are many ways of skinning this particular Presbyterian cat.

. *Ron Ferguson*
ORKNEY

This book is dedicated to
The congregations of
St George's and St Peter's, Easterhouse, Glasgow
and St Magnus Cathedral, Orkney
good listeners, good friends
and good companions on The Way

———— ✳ ————

PART I

Sermons

CHAPTER 1

The Singing Right Foot

Spike Milligan tells a story about a man who was on the top deck of a double-decker bus. Suddenly, he heard the sound of singing, and assumed it was one of the passengers. When the top deck emptied, he discovered that the singing was still going on, and that it was coming from himself!

Closer examination revealed that the voice was coming from his own right foot. He was very embarrassed, as more and more people came on the bus. What should he do? He decided to tie his bootlace tighter – but all that happened was that the voice became falsetto. He rushed downstairs, past the driver, his right foot singing all the while.

His troubles were not over, however. His right foot kept singing as he rushed along the street, past startled pedestrians. He had to mime the words to make it seem as if he was singing normally, and eventually reached home a nervous wreck.

As the days went by, he began to realise the potential of his new discovery. His right foot made a hit record, and went on tour. To cut a long story short, his right foot held a press conference, attended by pressmen from all over the world, and at it the man shot his foot in a fit of jealousy.

WHAT a delightful parable of the kingdom of God ...

The kingdom of God is not something we can build: it's something we receive. It's the kind of arena where your right foot bursts out singing 'Alleluias', and you've no control over it.

All we ever have are experiences and stories. Theologians try to sort

3

them out in a consistent way, and bring in grand names like 'Revelation', and 'Eschatology', but they're only ever partially successful. Experiences and stories can never make consistent theology, no matter how hard you try, and no matter how many grand Greek words you bring in.

A great deal of systematic theology seems to be about taming and controlling unruly material, and in the process squeezing the dangerously exciting lifeblood out of it. That's what Lawrence Durrell means when he says: 'Theology is very old ice cream, very tame sausage.' Compare that with how Delmore Schwartz describes poetry: 'Quick as tigers, clever as cats, vivid as oranges.'

Stories are very powerful. Let me tell you one.

The great Jewish rabbi, Baal Shem-Tov, used to go into a forest to meditate whenever misfortune threatened his community. There he would light a fire, and say a special prayer, and the misfortune would be averted.

Later, one of his disciples used to go to the same place in the forest for the same reason, and he would pray: 'Master of the Universe, listen! I do not know how to light the fire, but I am still able to say the prayer.' And again, a miracle would happen.

Still later, another disciple would go into the forest and say: 'I don't know how to light the fire. I don't know the prayer, but I know the place, and this must be sufficient.' Sure enough, the miracle happened again.

Even later, Rabbi Israel of Rizhin was asked to avert misfortune. He sat in his armchair with his head in his hands and said to God: 'I cannot even find the place in the forest. All I can do is to tell the story, and this must be sufficient.' And it was.

Stories have power. The Gaelic language has a word, *Seannachie*, which means story-teller – the bard who tells stories to the community, with great vividness and power – and his stories help to give the community its identity as they are repeated and repeated.

The Old Testament is full of powerful stories, told around the camp fires of Israel. Stories of Adam and Eve, Cain and Abel, Noah, Abraham, Isaac, Jacob, Samuel, Saul, David and Goliath: told again and again and again, shaping the community, helping it to understand its existence – powerful, life-giving stories.

Jesus was a *Seannachie*, a story-teller. He knew the power of story to illumine, and bring to a decision. As he sat round the campfires with the foundation of the new Israel, his disciple-friends, he told them story after story. We call them parables. And he would repeat them, time after time. The Sermon on the Mount was not simply one sermon that was preached once. These sayings of Jesus, full of vivid imagery, were uttered again and again until they were lodged in his disciples' brains: and they couldn't get these stories and sayings out of their minds.

Do you remember as a child, people telling you stories? It was magic. You'd ask for them again and again and again, the same ones. The disciples, I'm sure, were the same with Jesus. The stories he told were brilliant.

'C'mon Jesus,' you can imagine them saying, 'tell us again the story of the man with the two sons.'

Let's hear that story again, in a new version, in *A Glasgow Bible* ...'

Jesus told a story aboot a man who had two sons.

The younger wan said tae his faither, 'Hey faither, kin ah ask ye a favour? Why no gie me ma share o the faimily gear right noo, tae save me waitin till yer deid?'

The faither wis hurt, but agreed, an split his property between the two sons. A wee while efter, the younger son picked up aw his gear an left hame for the bright lights an the big city.

It wisny lang afore he wasted his hale fortune oan the bevvy, an the parties, an livin it up. Jist when he wis hittin rock bottom, a terrible famine swept ower the country. He needed work right bad, but aw he cud get wis a job wi a fermer, feedin the pigs. He wis so famished that he cud've fair eaten the beans the pigs were scoffin. Naebody took pity oan him.

Finally he gets wise an says tae himsel, 'Ach, ah'm aff ma heid, so I am – at hame even ma faither's servants are weel looked efter, an here's me stervin. Ah'll jist need tae bottle ma pride an go hame. Ah'll confess tae ma faither that ah've done wrang an ask him tae sign me up alang wi the servants.'

So he gets up an sterts oot for hame. He's still a lang wey fae his hoose when his faither catches sight o him an runs oot tae meet him. He throws his airms aroon his son an kisses him.

The boy wis greetin, 'Ah'm sorry faither – honest! Ah'm jist a loser an no fit tae be cawd yer son.'

But his faither shouted tae the servants, 'Fetch oot some nice clean claes for ma boy, an a ring for his finger – aye, an ah want ye tae kill the prize calf. Wir gauny hiv oorsels a real celebration this night!'

Noo the big brither wis comin in fae the fields. When he came near the hoose, he heard the music an jiggin. He cawd tae wan o the servants an asked whit wis up.

'Yer wee brither's come back hame, sir,' he wis telt. 'Aye, an we're celebratin like. Yer faither has even killt the prize coo for the feast.'

The big brither wis beelin – an widny go inty the hoose. So the faither comes oot tae reason wi him.

He answers his faither, 'Noo, haud oan an listen tae me. Ah've slaved for ye aw thae years an ye didny even wance gie a party for me. An noo that wee nyaff comes back! Been oan the randan, so he has! Spent aw yer money oan booze an hooers! An ye kill yer best coo for him?!'

The faither wis hurt at aw this. 'Ma son,' he says tae him, 'ye've aye been here wi me. Ye must ken that aw that's mine is yours. But ye see, it wis right tae celebrate. Ah thought ma son wis deid – an he's come back tae life. He wis lost – an noo he's come hame.'

When we hear that luminous story, we know all we need to know about God. He's like a father who sees his errant boy on the horizon and runs after him and throws his arms around him and kisses him.

And when we hear again the story of the Passion, of the Cross of Christ, and put it together with the story of the Prodigal Son, we realise it's the same kind of thing we're talking about. The same kind of G-O-D.

We're talking about a personal love, deep, deep at the heart of this universe; we're talking about a blood-red love that will never let us go, ever.

But can we prove it? Can we prove these stories are true? No, we can't. We can only live them. Experiences and stories: that's all we have: and that's more than enough to be getting on with. The problem is, we want to have everything pinned down, cut and dried: but, quite simply, we can't. The Bible is a mass of stories and experiences, a wonderfully chaotic mass, and there's no way we can make an entirely consistent theology out of it, thank God. The Bible is a glorious treasury, a rich kaleidoscope of images, a divine story book – but consistent it definitely isn't. The stories about God clash with each other, and overlap.

At one point God is described as being asleep; at another, he rises early in the morning; at yet another he is described as the one who neither slumbers nor sleeps. And so on. The Bible is gloriously inconsistent, story piled upon story, metaphor upon metaphor, image upon image, and we can only make it consistent by being very, very selective – like a film producer who leaves most of the inconvenient footage on the cutting room floor.

The difficulty is this: how do we talk about God, who is a mystery, when all we have is human speech? All we can do is open ourselves to experience and tell stories. What we mustn't do is pretend that these stories are literally true at every point: or say that God is literally a father, literally male, literally a rock, literally asleep, or literally anything. Our language is too fragile for that.

Theologians want to tidy everything up, but it can't be done. The fact that we have so many denominations and so many theologies all claiming biblical warrant shows that it can't be done. They all leave too much inconvenient material lying on the cutting room floor.

This would simply be entertaining if it weren't so dangerous. There are people who will kill those with whom they disagree. There are people who claim to know much more than they are entitled to claim and they will kill, or exclude, for the sake of tidiness.

As Professor Robert Carroll puts it:

If the definition of the divine is to include that which is beyond human comprehension, then any account of God which knows as much as traditional religions claim to know about such a being offends against that principle. Creeds and confessions, Bibles and Korans, all appear to be able to specify the inside-leg measurements of their god to such a degree of accuracy that they can persecute and prosecute any who differ from them in any detail. Religious history is filled with the corpses of people who knew less about the god than the creeds or sacred books permitted, or who knew other than was asserted in such sources.[2]

Does this mean that we don't know anything about God? No. We have experiences and stories: and some experiences and stories are more helpful than others. And we can testify to the fact that the stories of Jesus Christ – his birth, life, teaching, healing, dying and rising again, not only have power to illumine our lives, but to *change* them. When His story becomes interwoven with our story, things can never be the same. Some experiences and stories are life-changing and transforming.

The Spirit blows where it wills, and we can't control that. Remember the man whose right foot burst out singing ... when we try to control or manipulate or institutionalise the Spirit, we end up shooting ourselves in the foot.

Pentecost is the story of a Spirit which blows where it wants; and about a community of experience and story.

Someone has outlined the perennial Christian strategy as follows:

1   Gather the folks
2   Break the bread
3   Tell the stories

I began with a story, Let me close with a Hassidic tale passed on by the great Jewish theologian Martin Buber.

My grandfather was paralysed. Once he was asked to tell a story about his teacher, and he told how the holy Baal Shem Tov used to jump and dance when he was praying. My grandfather stood up when he was telling the story, and the story carried him away so much that he had to jump and dance to show how the master had done it. From that moment he was healed.

That is what Pentecostal parables are all about.

---

1   Jamie Stuart: *A Glasgow Bible* (Edinburgh: Saint Andrew Press, 1997).
2   Robert Carroll: *Wolf in the Sheepfold* (London: SPCK, 1991).

CHAPTER 2

The Ministry
of Silly Walks

OF all the stories in the Bible, surely the most gloriously shambolic is that of the birth of the Christian Church. It is confusing, disturbing and messy. It's real 'heidbanger' stuff. And yet you can sense it right away: something amazing is happening. Here is Luke's version of the events (Acts 2: 1-21, Revised Standard Version):

When the day of Pentecost had come, they were all together in one place. And suddenly a sound came from heaven like the rush of a mighty wind, and it filled all the house where they were sitting. And there appeared to them tongues as of fire, distributed and resting on each one of them. And they were all filled with the Holy Spirit and began to speak in other tongues, as the Spirit gave them utterance.

Now there were dwelling in Jerusalem Jews, devout men from every nation under heaven. And at this sound the multitude came together, and they were bewildered, because each one heard them speaking in his own language. And they were amazed and wondered, saying, 'Are not all these who are speaking Galileans? And how is it that we hear, each of us in his own native language? Parthians and Medes and Elamites and residents of Mesopotamia, Judea and Cappadocia, Pontus and Asia, Phrygia and Pamphylia, Egypt and the parts of Libya belonging to Cyrene, and visitors from Rome, both Jews and proselytes, Cretans and Arabians, we hear them telling in our own tongues the mighty works of God'. And all were amazed and perplexed, saying to one another, 'What does this mean?' But others mocking said, 'They are filled with new wine'.

But Peter, standing with the eleven, lifted up his voice and addressed them, 'Men of Judea and all who dwell in Jerusalem, let this be known to you, and give ear to my words. For these men are not drunk, as you suppose, since it is only the third hour of the day; but this is what was spoken by the prophet Joel:

"And in the last days it shall be, God declares,
that I will pour out my Spirit upon all flesh,
and your sons and your daughters shall prophesy,
and your young men shall see visions,
and your old men shall dream dreams;
yea, and on my menservants and my maidservants in those days
I will pour out my Spirit; and they shall prophesy.
And I will show wonders in the heaven above
and signs on the earth beneath,
blood, and fire, and vapour of smoke;
the sun shall be turned into darkness
and the moon into blood,
before the day of the Lord comes,
the great and manifest day.
And it shall be that whoever calls on the name of the Lord
shall be saved."'

What on earth – or in heaven – is going on here in the midst of this Pentecostal madhouse? Has everyone gone crazy? Or are they just drunk?

That's what some of the bystanders suggested – that the disciples were drunk. Peter, ever the practical man, stands up and says: 'These people are not drunk, as you suppose; it is only nine o'clock in the morning.' Nice touch that. What this great Prince of the Church is saying, roughly, is: They can't be drunk – the Palestinian off-licences haven't opened yet. Trust big Peter to get right to the heart of things.

This birthday of the Christian Church is pretty zany stuff, really. Those of us who belong to the Church would do well to remember that. There's something essentially batty about us, despite our respectable front. Every time we, as the Church, get up to lecture the nation we should think about that, and maybe sit down again.

All we have, remember, are experiences and stories. We hardly have the language to describe what's happening to us when we encounter the divine. We have clues: and stories like the Prodigal Son tell us that what we are dealing with is a lover, a being who will not let us go. So, what is being talked about is not a sentimental kind of love. Sometimes it's a harsh and dreadful love; and now and again this loving God seems like the slavering Hound of the Baskervilles.

People often think that to meet the divine being must be a soft, gentle encounter: but to fall into the hands of the living God can sometimes feel more like being mugged up a close by a dark and mysterious stranger.

Prayer is our stumbling attempt to communicate with this divine lover, this Stranger who does unwise things like stretching across a beam of wood and letting people hammer nails into his hands and feet. Peace is his gift to us, but it's a disturbing peace, the kind of peace that can keep you awake at night. And he asks us to live out that peace, to provide alternatives to the ways of violence in today's world. This is a kind of divine madness, and every time we're tempted to present Christianity as purely rational, or the height of common-sense, we should read the story of the birth of the Christian Church three times a day after meals.

Yes, all we have are experiences and stories. What stories they are! What is the story of Pentecost saying to us?

One of the things the story of Pentecost tells us is that the Church is, well, weird. The nuttiness co-efficient is pretty high. Clergy dress up in robes and cassocks and mitres and make portentous statements about the Will of God and the state of the world; or maybe we dress down, into jeans and trainers, and wave our hands in the air, and pretend we're more Pentecostal than thou. Whatever we do, it's a bit of a nonsense. We have grave debates among the churches about who has the right form of ministry – but sometimes it seems that what we have in common is the Ministry of Silly Walks.

Yet one of the ways in which God would appear to work in the world is through this same nutty, divine, institution. There's a legend about Jesus, after his Ascension, meeting the Archangel Michael. Michael asks Jesus what plans he has made to carry on his work on earth. Jesus says that he has left Peter and John and James and the others to do it. The archangel is aghast, in the way that only archangels can be aghast. 'What back-up plans do you have if they let you down?' is the anxious question. 'I have no other plans,' says Jesus, quietly ...

Scary!

Meanwhile, back at the Pentecostal ranch, Peter, who comes over as a cross between Moses and the comedian John Cleese, quietens the bedlam of everyone shouting in different tongues. He not only points out that his friends aren't drunk, he goes on to preach a spell-binder. He tells stories. He takes some of the stories of the Hebrew scriptures, and shows how they overlap with the story of the death and resurrection of Jesus. And in the process of telling these stories, peoples lives are changed.

He takes it back to the prophecy of Joel (Acts 2: 17):

And in the last days it shall be, God declares,
that I will pour out my Spirit upon all flesh,
and your sons and your daughters shall prophesy,
and your young men shall see visions,
and your old men will dream dreams.

What is happening here is the birth of a community where spirit and bread and dreams and visions are shared: between young and old; between men and women. The spirit is poured out on all of them, equally.

In such a community, in such a wounded, crazy community, it is possible to learn how to pray. It is possible to learn how to work for peace. It is possible to learn how to talk about G-O-D. Within such a community you can gather the folks; break the bread; and tell the stories. Within such a community, it's possible to learn new things.

It's possible ... but something has gone wrong, hasn't it? Somewhere along the line the Church has surrendered what Paul calls 'the glorious liberty of the children of God' – surrendered its birthright for a mess of respectability and conformity and rectitude. How often have our churches been accused of being drunk, for heaven's sake? We're far too sober by half, too sober for our own good.

And we have surrendered the beautiful Pentecostal equality of men and women, of sisters and brothers in the spirit, for a half-baked unassailable male authority. Mary has been very quickly sent back to join Martha in the ecclesiastical kitchen, barefoot and pregnant.

There's something very radical and dangerous about Pentecost. In turning our back upon it, we have opted for safety and control, and a much quieter and more ordered life. We've tried to turn the wine back into water. We've tried to switch the colour back to the old black and white. And we've swallowed the line that there's no such thing as society or no such thing as community, that things have to be this way because things have to be this way.

No wonder we have to tranquillise ourselves to deal with our own despair.

But the Spirit keeps breaking through. Subversive characters, like Martin Luther King, keep insisting that things don't have to be the way they are: they keep dreaming dreams about spirit-empowered possibilities, about alternatives …

I have a dream that one day this nation will rise up and live out the true meaning of its creed – we hold these truths to be self-evident, that all men are created equal.

I have a dream that one day on the red hills of Georgia, the sons of former slaves and the sons of former slave-owners will be able to sit down together at the table of brotherhood.

I have a dream that one day, even the state of Mississippi, a state sweltering with the heat of injustice, sweltering with the heat of oppression, will be transformed into an oasis of freedom and justice.

I have a dream that my four little children will one day live in a nation where they will not be judged by the colour of their skin but by the content on their character. I have a dream today!

I have a dream that one day down in Alabama, with its vicious racists, with its governor having his lips dripping with the words of interposition and nullification, one day, right there in Alabama, little black boys and black girls will be able to join hands with little white boys and white girls as sisters and brothers. I have a dream today!

I have a dream that one day every valley shall be exalted, every hill and mountain shall be made low, the rough places will be made plain and the crooked places will be made straight, and the glory of the Lord shall be revealed and all flesh shall see it together.[1]

This is the divine madness. Pentecost is about keeping alive the dream, until that day when the loving Stranger, who insists on calling us his friends, returns with nail prints in his transfigured and translucent hands ... until that day, beyond pain and death, when we shall gather all the folks, break the bread, and tell the beautiful stories.

---

1   Taken from a public speech by Martin Luther King. Text from David J Garrow: *Bearing the Cross* (London: Vintage, 1993).

CHAPTER 3

It wisnae me

The man said, 'The woman whom thou gavest to be with me, she gave me fruit of the tree, and I ate.'

Genesis 3: 12

WHEN I was a minister in a big housing scheme in Glasgow some years ago, I looked out of the upstairs window of our house and saw a couple of urchins throwing stones at our living room window. They weren't singling us out – they were simply having a bit of sport, as they did with all the people in the street.

I rushed out and got hold of the boys, demanding: 'Why did you do that?'

They replied with one voice, almost like a Greek chorus: 'It wisnae me!'

I had a morning ritual of looking out of the upstairs window to check if my battered Ford Cortina Mark II was still parked outside. One day I saw a boy standing cheerfully on the bonnet of the car. He was attempting to detach one of the windscreen wipers. I ran downstairs, and followed him to his home. When his mother came to the door, I told her what had happened. She simply stood there, looked me straight in the eye, and said: 'It wisnae him.'

At that point, there was no further point in human discourse. All basis for mutual discussion had gone.

I'm reminded of the story of the school chaplain taking a school assembly on the subject of the Battle of Jericho.

'Who was responsible for knocking down the walls of Jericho?' he asked the class.

The response from one of the boys was automatic. 'It wisnae me,' he protested.

The great city of Glasgow has a coat of arms reflecting the story of Saint Mungo. It is accompanied by the pious motto 'Let Glasgow flourish by the preaching of His Word and the praising of His Name'. A less romantic and more accurate emblem would be a picture of two wee boys with stones in their hands, above the immortal words: 'It wisnae me.'

When I played football with my small sons, I encouraged them, when brought down by a dubious tackle, to cry 'penalty!' automatically. [This was so that twenty years later, when they were brought down in the English penalty area in injury time ....]

West of Scotland parents similarly install, 'It wisnae me.'

'It wisnae me' comes in many languages, many forms. The denial of responsibility is not a new thing. It's basic to the human condition. It's a natural human response to accusation and guilt, even when caught red-handed, stones in hands.

The response is as old as Adam.

Now the story of the Garden of Eden is not a gleaming presentation of literal, historical truth. Is it factual? Come on. Is it true? Yes. It's a brilliant, beautifully economic depiction of the root human condition.

I'm reminded of George MacLeod's observation that the trouble with the English is that they can't distinguish between facts and truth. A further deep complication is that we so often set myth and truth in opposition to each other. To insist that they must be opposites is a form of literary and philosophical barbarism. To say that the Garden of Eden story is a myth is not the same as saying that it is untrue – like all high quality living myth it gives us more truth than we want to know.

So God tells Adam: 'You can eat from every tree in the garden, except the tree of the knowledge of good and evil – the day that you eat it you will die.'

Then along comes the snake. It's a magic, speaking snake. [Literally true? Are you sure?] It says to the woman: 'Did God really say that? No, you won't really die – in fact you'll be like God.'

So Eve eats the fruit, and enjoys it. She gives it to Adam, who also scoffs it. It tastes very, very good.

Then along comes God, out for an evening stroll in the garden. [Still advocating literalism?] 'Where are you, Adam?' he asks.

'I hid myself because I was naked,' says Adam.

'Who told you you were naked?' asks God. 'Have you been eating that fruit I told you not to touch?'

And Adam says, in his finest Hebrew: 'It wisnae me.' Not only does he say 'It wisnae me', he says 'It wisnae me, it was *the wife!*'

The spotlight turns on Eve. 'What have *you* been up to?'

Eve says – surprise, surprise – 'It wisnae me.' Not only does she say 'It wisnae me', she adds 'It wisnae me, it was *the snake!*'

Exit magic speaking snake, strangely mute, on left.

* * *

Is this a true story? Well, no … well, yes. It's all there, isn't it? The whole Bible is a catalogue of stories of people saying, in one way or another, 'It wisnae me'.

Cain kills Abel. God interrogates him about what has happened. Cain says: 'It wisnae me. I'm not my brother's keeper.'

And so on, and so on. All the way through the story of Israel, all the way through the story of the New Testament.

The classic example, which can stand for all the rest, is the story of Peter.

'Jesus,' he tells his master, 'you can count on me, big Peter. No problem.'

Jesus knows Peter better than he knows himself. 'Peter,' he says, 'before the cock crows twice, you will deny me three times.'

'Not me Lord,' says Peter.

And when Jesus is betrayed, the servant girl says to Peter, 'Haven't I seen you before, big man? You were with Jesus.'

And Peter says – *all together now* – 'It wisnae me.'

In fact, he tries to cover up his rough Galilean accent. He says, with a Palestinian bool in his mooth, 'It was not I.'

Exit Peter on left, weeping bitterly.

* * *

Then Jesus is taken away. Pilate interrogates him about the charges before him.

And Jesus says: 'It wisnae ... '

No, he disnae. He doesn't. He does not.

He is silent.

The irony is that the one man in human history who is entitled to say 'It wisnae me', stands dumb before his accusers. And it's his accusers who have the stones and the weapons in their hands.

What an amazing drama is this drama of our salvation!

In this season of Lent, we have been following Jesus on his way to Jerusalem and the Cross. We have been travelling with him in his times of temptation and testing – as the shape of his Messiahship becomes clear.

You see, he is our Representative. He is the shape of the new humanity, a new kind of human being, and he walks that way for us. And in so doing, he provides a remedy for the human condition.

As the first letter of Peter puts it:

For to this you have been called, because Christ also suffered for you, leaving you an example, that you should follow in his steps. He committed no sin; no guile was found on his lips. When he was reviled, he did not revile in return; when he suffered, he did not threaten; but he trusted to him who judges justly. He himself bore our sins in his body on the tree, that we might die to sin and live to righteousness. By his wounds you have been healed.

We can't expect to get our minds around all of this. But the freedom Christ brings to us is this: when we are accused, instead of saying 'It wisnae me', we can say – 'Yes, it *was* me'. Part of being grown up is to say, 'Yes, it was me', even if it was a terrible thing. To say this is not necessarily a safeguard against ever doing another terrible thing; but we can take responsibility precisely because we stand in freedom fields.

We don't need any more to blame the Catholics or the Protestants or the English or the Irish or the Muslims or the Hindus or the Jews or the Arabs – or even the weather – for everything that goes wrong in our lives.

We can stand and say 'Yes, it was me', knowing that we are free people, part of the new humanity in Christ. We can let the stones fall from our hands and welcome the liberation of God.

* * *

In Iona abbey, right in front of the communion table, there is an old Persian carpet. A story that George MacLeod used to tell about the carpet – and, of course, all stories by George MacLeod are true, are they not? – is that it came from the court of a Persian prince. On it, there is a place for the judge, a place for the prosecutor and a place for the accused.

It's right that it should be placed in front of the communion table. God in Christ is the one who accuses us. God in Christ is the one who judges us. God in Christ is the one who takes our place, and tells us to go home. For home is God.

And that, precisely and dramatically, is why the Gospel is not Good Advice, but Good News.

CHAPTER 4

Love your
Crooked Neighbour

But Jacob said to Rebekah his mother, 'Behold, my brother Esau is a hairy man, and I am a smooth man'.

Genesis 27: 11

But God demonstrates his own love towards us, in that while we were yet sinners, Christ died for us.

Romans 5: 8

BY any standards, Jacob was an out and out swine. Let's just remind ourselves of his great moral accomplishments.

He twice cheated his twin brother Esau out of his inheritance. The first time, remember, Esau comes in from the fields, starving. Jacob, it so happens, is cooking some food. It smells good.

Esau is not exactly the Brain of Israel – in fact, there was no Israel yet. There was no sign of a brain yet, either. Esau is crying out for betrayal, and his slightly younger brother is just the man to oblige him.

'Give me that food!' cries Esau. 'I'll give you anything you want for it.'

Jacob can hardly believe his luck. He knows what he wants – Esau's birthright, as the eldest child. For the sake of some bread and lentils, Esau gives away his most precious heritage – the birthright of a first-born son.

Not content with filching the birthright from his daft brother, Jacob wants his father's blessing as well – the blessing due to the eldest son. So, aided and abetted by his scheming mother, he cheats both Esau and Isaac.

Isaac is old, and his sight is failing. He tells Esau that he would dearly love to eat a savoury meal of meat, and would then bless Esau before he died. So Esau goes off to the hills to hunt game.

'Go to the flock,' Rebekah tells Jacob, 'and bring two choice kids and I will make a savoury meal for your father. Cover your hands with hairy skins, so that when your father comes back he will think you are Esau and give you his blessing. Go quickly, before your brother comes back.'

There is something horribly fascinating about what comes next.

'Here am I,' says Jacob, putting on a special voice. 'I am Esau, your son. Here is the food. Give me your blessing.'

Now Isaac may be blind and decrepit, but he is not a fool. He realises that the voice sounds suspiciously like Jacob's.

'Come near, my son,' he says to Jacob, 'so that I may be sure that you really are Esau.'

Now Esau was a hairy man. We all know that, from our Sunday school days. We watch from the sidelines as Jacob goes forward with the skins covering his smooth hands. We want to shout, like the audience in a pantomime – 'Look out Isaac! You're being tricked!'

The story-teller of Genesis is a master of his craft. We watch, with bated breath.

'Your voice is the voice of Jacob,' says Isaac, 'but your hands are the hands of Esau. Are you really Esau?'

'I am,' says Jacob.

'Come here and kiss me,' says Isaac.

Jacob, prefiguring Judas Iscariot, kisses his father.

Isaac smells the tang of the fields, the smell of Esau, the worker. So he blesses Jacob, believing him to be Esau.

Audience groans.

Exit Jacob on left, with a satisfied smile on his face. You see, in Hebrew theology, the blessing, once given, cannot be revoked. And the blessing is no empty thing – it brings certain property benefits.

Enter the luckless, hairy, Esau on right, carrying a steaming plate of savoury food, and puts it before his father.

'Who are you?' asks Isaac.

'I am your first-born son, Esau,' replies his dutiful son.

Even the stupid Esau realises that he has been well and truly had again by his crafty younger brother. Jacob is now Esau's master.

So Esau decides to kill his brother, but the quick-footed Jacob leaves town fast. As he heads for hills, he realises that there is no one after him. He feels safe enough to lie down at night to sleep, and he uses a stone for a pillow.

Jacob doesn't toss and turn with a guilty conscience, but goes into a deep sleep. And he dreams: he dreams that there is a ladder reaching from earth to heaven, with angels running up and down on it. Then he hears a voice saying to him:

'I am the Lord, the God of Abraham and Isaac. The land on which you lie I will give to you and your descendants. In you and your descendants all the nations of the earth shall be blessed. I will be with you and protect you wherever you go. I will not forsake you.'

Here is a man who would have sold his grannie to get what he wanted being told that he is going to be a source of blessing for future generations. Jacob has not got his just deserts. As the American writer Frederick Buechner puts it:

It wasn't Holy Hell that God gave him, in other words, but Holy Heaven, not to mention the marvellous lesson thrown in for good measure. The lesson was, needless to say, that even for a dyed-in-the-wool, double-barrelled con artist like Jacob there are a few things in this world you can't get but can only be given, and one of these things is love in general, and another is the love of God in particular.[1]

Jacob wakes from his dream, shocked.

'Surely the Lord is in this place,' he concludes, 'and I didn't know it. How awesome is this place! This is none other than the house of God, and this is the gate of heaven.'

The bold Jacob goes to look for a wife. He sees his cousin, the lovely Rachel, and decides to marry her. His crafty uncle Laban – it seems to run in the family – gets him to work for him for seven years, and then he cheats Jacob by substituting Rachel's sister Leah on his wedding night. Jacob then has to work another seven years to marry Rachel.

What an incredible Old Testament soap opera this is! Every episode gets crazier. There are all sorts of dubious goings-on with hand-maidens, and at the last count Jacob is the father of twelve children. Imagine what the tabloids would have made of Jacob!

Things can only get worse, and they do. Jacob double-crosses his double-crossing father-in-law by conning him out of a good part of his livestock, and then sneaking away with most of the family silver.

As he is heading homeward, another amazing thing happens to Jacob. He has a very strange experience. As he is preparing to cross over the river Jabbok, a man wrestles him till the break of day. No one wins the contest, but Jacob is lamed in the struggle.

Jacob says to the mysterious stranger: 'I will not let you go until you bless me.'

The stranger says: 'Your name shall no longer be Jacob, but Israel, for you have struggled with God and with men, and have prevailed.'

The stranger then refuses to give Jacob his name, but blesses him.

Jacob is awestruck, and says, 'I have seen God face to face, and my life is preserved.'

Jacob then heads for home, but to get there he has to go through the territory of his brother Esau. He expects Esau and his men to kill him, and so he sends an advance party with all kinds of gifts to appease him.

What happens next is extraordinary. Esau runs towards Jacob, not to kill him, but to embrace him. He has forgiven his swindling brother.

* * *

This is a totally astonishing sequence of stories. Jacob is a con man and a cheat. He's not the kind of man anyone – other than Esau – would have wanted to buy a used camel from. ('Honest, sir, it's only done 20,000 cubits. It's been well looked after. Had only one owner, an elderly spinster from Beersheba.')

You could picture him today in a very sharp suit with a mobile phone, making dubious deals and cheating people all over the place. He truly is a smooth man, in every sense of the word.

What is all the more remarkable is that the swine we are talking about is the Father of Israel, the people of God. How are we to understand this? We can't even reframe it by saying that after he met God, he was converted, lived a blameless life, and went on a tour of the Middle East giving his testimony. No. According to the story, he continued to double-cross, even after his first meeting with God.

This story is deeply offensive to us. It is confusing. Our problem is that we want God to work only through good and moral people. But life is not as simple as that. Nor, apparently is God. In fact, in the biblical story, he seems almost to collude with Jacob!

We cannot accuse God of having no sense of morality – ('I don't know about you, God, but I've got my standards!'). I suspect that God has a sense of humour, too – (the great Trickster in the Sky further rattles the moral cages by perversely choosing Moses the murderer, and David the adulterer, and they don't follow the classic conversion scripts either). We want to turn religion simply into a code of ethics, but God will not let us. It is about something else, something deeper.

The story of Jacob upsets our notion of a tidy and predictable God who only works through good people. We do all kinds of handstands to make it fit our preconceived categories. One minister who was preaching on the story really got his theological knickers into a twist. He talked about how fine a man Esau was, and only when he got to the end did he remember that, after all, God's promise went to Jacob.

'My friends,' roared the preacher, 'after so adjudging the character of the worthy Esau you may be wondering why it was that Providence made his choice of Jacob. But ye must aye remember that in that choice Providence was acting in His official capacity, and may have felt forced to do that which, on personal grounds, he would surely have resisted.'

Providence acting in 'His official capacity'. Isn't that delicious!
Buechner again:

*Luckily for Jacob, God doesn't love people because of who they are
but because of who he is. 'It's on the house' is one way of saying it, and
'it's by grace' is another, just as it was by grace that it was Jacob of
all people who became not only the father of the twelve tribes of Israel
but the many times great grandfather of Jesus of Nazareth, and just as
it was by grace that Jesus of Nazareth was born into this world at
all.*[2]

This everyday story of Jewish country folk is deeply offensive to
us, and no theological gymnastics can turn it into a morality tale with
a happy ending. It's the guy with the black hat who wins the lottery.
Why Jacob became the Father of Israel is a divine mystery, as are so
many things in life. It is possibly even a divine joke.

The offence in the story lies in the fact that we want the baddies
to get their deserts. We, of course, identify with the goodies. It's
exactly the same offence that lies at the heart of the stories of the
Prodigal Son, and the Labourers in the Vineyard.

These are all stories about radical grace. Our Christian faith is not
about morality in the first instance, but about undeserved love. It turns
our categories upside down.

Will Campbell was a Southern Baptist minister who was a leader
in the civil rights movement in the States. He slowly and reluctantly
came to the realisation that God loved the Ku Klux Klan members
every bit as much as he loved the right-on, progressive civil rights
people. After the murder of one of the very peaceable civil rights
campaigners, Will Campbell was asked by the local newspaper editor,
an atheist, to give him a definition of Christianity in less than ten
words. Campbell thought for a bit, then replied: 'We're all bastards,
but God loves us anyway.'

That's not quite how Augustine or Aquinas or John Calvin or any
of the other great theologians would have put it, but that's roughly
what they meant. The gospel story is about a lover-god who wants to

turn us from enemies into friends, and like all good lovers is prepared to pay the price. *But God demonstrates his own love towards us, in that while we were yet sinners, Christ died for us.*

Christ didn't die for us or offer us his life *after* we had repented. As George MacLeod has put it: 'We have been given union with God, whether we like it or not, know it or not, want it or not. Our flesh is his flesh, and we can't jump out of our skins. It isn't pantheism. It is a free spontaneous gift of the living God. And it happened for everyone.'

* * *

Here is the heart and core of the matter. God's love is unconditional. It is offered to all people, no matter their background, or past history. It is indiscriminating, Jesus says: *God makes his sun rise on the evil and the good, and sends rain on the just and the unjust.*

The Hebrew people started off as slaves, outcasts. God's love liberated them, and they danced the dance of freedom. But then some of them began to believe God loved them because they were good. They began to feel that they deserved God's love, they had *earned* it, they had a claim upon God. If God loved them because they were good, then God must hate those who were bad.

And soon the righteous people began to define who was good and who was bad; who were clean and who were unclean; who were insiders and who were outsiders. They began to judge other people, and categorise them, and demonise them.

God does not love us because we are good, but simply because he loves us. This is the source of our true security.

When we look honestly in the mirror, we see someone who is a mixture of good and bad, sometimes wearing a white hat, sometimes wearing a black hat. And God loves us even when we wear the black hat. Even when we break his heart. Even when we choose to be his enemies.

And he comes for us in love: He comes for us, those who think they're good, and those who know they're bad. And his love is for all humankind without reservation.

But God demonstrates his own love towards us, in that while we were yet sinners, Christ died for us. All of us. Equally.

* * *

One final thing: If God loves us all, and if God sends the sun and the rain on the just and the unjust, why should we bother to be good at all?

We are good not in order to worm our way into God's good books, but because He loves us, and we want to respond to him, to this lover-God, and to be like him.

And to be like him, says Jesus, you are to love your enemies. Not just your pals, your cronies, your families, your best friends. Your enemies.

We've to stop separating people into the white hats and the black hats. We simply don't know enough about the inner stories of people to set ourselves up as judges. I love the words of W H Auden:

O stand, stand at the window
As the tears scald and start;
You shall love your crooked neighbour
With your crooked heart.[3]

And the invitation to this table is to all of us, without qualification. This bread, this wine. It's for sinners, for broken people, for people with crooked hearts. That means you and me.

At this table, we may be gifted with an encounter with a divine Stranger who lames us and blesses us. *Surely the Lord is in this place, and I didn't know it. How awesome is this place! This is none other than the house of God, and this is the gate of heaven.*

He took the bread and broke it, and said Take, eat, this is my body which is for you. And he took the cup, saying This is my blood which is shed for you,

All of you.

The white hats and the black hats.

The good, the bad and the ugly.

The Lord opens his hands to give you what you need. And when you examine the hands that offer you what you need, you'll see that they have nailprints on them.

The bread is broken for you, even when you break his heart.

The wine is poured for you, even when you are at your most perverse.

Take it.

It's for you.

Then go home dancing – with a limp.

1   Frederick Buechner: *Peculiar Treasures* (London: Harper & Row, 1979).
2   ibid.
3   From W H Auden: 'As I walked out one Evening' in *Collected Shorter Poems* (London: Faber, 1966).

CHAPTER 5

Prayer and the Missionary Position

But God shows his love for us in that while we were yet sinners Christ died for us.

Romans 5: 8

When you pray, go into your room and shut the door and pray to your father who is in secret; and your father who sees in secret will reward you.

Matthew 6: 6

AT a Scottish cathedral some years ago it was decided to make an experiment. The minister felt that there should be a place in the cathedral for daily private prayer and meditation, and he decided to set aside one of the side chapels for that purpose. The Kirk Session were a bit suspicious about what seemed to some of them to be a Roman Catholic tendency, but they found it difficult to argue against the proposal.

The beadle was a guardian of all things Presbyterian, and he decided to keep a close watch on the proceedings. After the first week of the side chapel's new function, the minister asked the beadle if anyone had made use of the new facility.

'Aye,' the beadle muttered darkly, 'I caught two of them at it this very mornin'.'

Prayer's not really a bad thing to be 'caught at'. What are the chances that you would be 'caught at it'? And if you were, would you be embarrassed about being caught in the act?

* * *

There's a certain mystique about prayer, isn't there? It's as if it were an activity for spiritual athletes, for specialists, for strange people who like that kind of thing. In fact, most people pray at some time or another, even if they only groan 'Oh God' when they're in trouble.

The trouble is that most people think they're not good at it, or not good enough for it, and so they give up.

Prayer is a bit like sex. With both activities, most practitioners secretly think that everyone else is much better at it, or having more fun with it than they are; and if only they could learn the latest exciting technique or position – rather than the old-fashioned, boring missionary position – or get the newest manual, the kingdom of heaven would be at hand. It's simply not true, either about making love or about prayer. (In fact, prayer is a form of love-making, but we'll come to that in a minute.)

Many of us ministers have a whole section of our bookshelves devoted to methods of prayer, but still can't pray. The prayer manuals – like sex manuals – can sometimes be more intimidating than helpful. All these damned exercises! You just achieve one stage; then you turn the page to find there's another ten stages to go – and when you attain that, you are told you are guilty of pride!

The trouble is that we often, in the name of piety, try to force ourselves back into a medieval frame. It doesn't work. Alternatively, we may become more modern and oriental, and try the lotus position, or deep breathing through alternate nostrils – and instead of becoming a Seventh Dan spiritual genius, we may end up being carted off to hospital, leg wrapped around the neck. Oh God! Sometimes these modern 'How to' books seem to have a hidden subtitle: 'How to feel even more inadequate.' Most of us need lessons in feeling inadequate like we need another committee on the future of the Church. We're already experts at giving ourselves a hammering in the name of God.

* * *

So where do we go from here, we who live in a post-modern age yet haven't even caught up with being modern?

Earlier I said that prayer was a form of making love. What prayer is for you depends very much on your notion of God. If you see God as a vengeful tyrant, your prayer will be an attempt to keep him off your back, maybe by bargaining with him – 'If you promise not to send me cancer, God, I'll go to church every week and say my prayers every day. Honest, I'll be very, very good.'

If you believe God to be a remote and distant being, prayer will be a long-distance contemplation which doesn't warm the heart.

If you see God as a divine schoolmaster, you'll provide essays every day in your prayers – words, words, words and ever more wearisome words. And you'll worry about whether you've got the right words, or enough words to ward off a blow from the great menacing Lochgelly in the sky.

If you see God as someone who plays cosmic dice, or who picks out one for heaven and ten for hell, a' for his glory, then your prayer will be a form of cowering, or of passive acceptance. A more human form of prayer would be to curse such a god.

But what if God is ... a lover?

I'm not talking here about romance. I'm not talking about Mills and Boon theology. I'm not talking about sentimentality. I'm not pretending God and ourselves are equal partners. I'm not talking about God as the pal next door who is addressed casually by trendy clergy as if he were a benevolent uncle – what George MacLeod called 'All-matey God'. I'm talking about the God Jesus Christ shows us – One whose essential nature is a burning love which is at the same time harsh and dreadful and passionate and tender. What if God is like that!

All talk of God is tentative and stumbling and provisional, because 'God' is the name for a mystery. That does not render us speechless, but it should make us very chaste with words about that ultimate mystery. All we have are experiences and stories and parables, and a human language which repeatedly breaks under the weight of divine Otherness. We need to beware of too many words, or of words which claim too much knowledge. As Robert Funk puts it: 'When the gods are silent, man becomes a gossip.'

We love, because he loved us first: that's how the scripture talks about the love relationship between God and humankind, which undergirds real prayer. What the stories, the parables point to is an experience of unconditional, burning love.

If we think that prayer is a way of climbing a ladder to God, then we'll never make it. If we get past stage one, we'll probably fall at stage two. And so on. Christianity is not about us ascending to God up a ladder of devotion, but about dealing with a God who has *descended*. Prayer is essentially response to a lover-God. *We have been given union with God whether we like it or not, know it or not, want it or not.*

And prayer is about communion with that lover-God. As with any love relationship, we need both words and silence – and presence, real listening – and symbols. Openness and receptiveness are lover-like qualities, too. And this is also where Protestants and Roman Catholics can learn from each other, and help each other along the way.

Are candles Protestant or Catholic? Neither, of course. They are symbols of light, and they can help us in our prayers. They can gently take some of the weight when our words break down. Those of us who are Protestants threw them out of our churches, and have been much the poorer ever since.

Is reading the Bible Protestant or Catholic? And what about the simplicity of a rosary? To hold a bead on the upstairs deck of a bus, while imagining a loved one in the presence of God, is good psychology and good prayer.

We could do with at least a little bit of Pentecostal anarchy, and get out of our institutional boxes. You can stand, sit, kneel, get into the lotus position, or do the handstand. It doesn't matter. God has a sense of humour. And you can pray anywhere – in church, on the top deck of a bus, walking in a park. It's certainly good to have a quiet space, even for a minute or two. Here is what Jesus said:

And when you pray, you must not be like the hypocrites; for they love to stand and pray in the synagogues and at the street corners, that they may be seen by men. Truly I say to you, they have their reward. But when you pray, go into your room and shut the door and pray to your father who is in secret; and your father who sees in secret will reward you.

Matthew 6: 5, 6

One woman with a family told me that the only time she gets any peace is when she goes to the loo. That's fine. You could create for yourself an ecumenical toilet with Bible, candle, rosary, devotional library. When people hammer on the door, you can use that as an audio-visual representation of battering on the doors of heaven. Why should teenagers have all the good toilets?

* * *

One last thing. Prayer is not just about deep breathing and self-fulfilment. It's about a new and radical way of seeing the world. It's about transformation. And if you begin to see the world through the eyes of Jesus, you may find yourself in trouble.

Prayer, says the Jesuit priest Daniel Berrigan, is a subversive activity.

Wouldn't it be marvellous if more of us were caught at it?

CHAPTER 6

Who do you think
you are?

What is man, that thou art mindful of him, and the son of man that thou dost care for him?

Psalm 8: 4

He said to them, 'But who do you say that I am?' Simon Peter replied, 'You are the Christ, the Son of the living God.'

Matthew 16: 15

SEVERAL years ago, you may remember, Hurricane Andrew hit the United States. It caused some devastation in Florida, and President George Bush, as politicians or heads of state usually do on such occasions, went down to talk to the people.

An old people's home had been hit by the edge of the hurricane, and many of the old people were understandably quite disorientated by the experience. President Bush went up to one elderly lady in a wheel chair and said to her: 'Do you know who I am?'

The old lady looked into his eyes, and after a few seconds she replied: 'If you don't know who you are, perhaps you should go to the Information Desk and ask there.'

If I were to ask you who you are this morning, you'd probably reply with your name, and where you come from. But the question from the Bible goes deeper than that: deeper than your name and where you come from. It asks: Who are you, what are you? What are you worth?

The Nazis had an answer to the question about the value of people. Human beings were taken to the prison camps. If they had any rings, the jewelry was taken off to be sold. After the Jews had been gassed, the gold fillings were removed from their teeth. Their hair was taken off for cushions. Some minerals were removed. Human being might be worth a couple of pounds.

And for those who ran some of the prisoner-of-war camps in Japan, human beings were cheap labour, to be tortured, brutalised and abused. Women were to be sexual objects for the Japanese army. *What is man, that thou art mindful of him?*

But all of this isn't just ancient history. In very recent times in Europe, if you were a Croat, or a Serb, or a Muslim, you counted for nothing to the opposition. You could be thrown out of your house, or raped or tortured or killed, simply because you were the enemy. You could be the victim of 'ethnic cleansing', just like the Jews. Worthless. On the scrap heap.

Or nearer home. In Ireland you could be bombed into little pieces, just because you happened to be a Protestant, or a Catholic. Ethnic cleansing.

The way you answer the question 'What is a human being?' or 'Who am I?' will determine how you live your life. It will certainly determine how you treat other people.

Some facts:

- The human heart beats about 100,000 times every 24 hours.
- The heart pumps six quarts of blood through over 96,000 miles of blood vessels – this is an equivalent of 6300 gallons being pumped every day – and if you live to be 50 your heart will have pumped 150 million gallons.
- That six quarts of blood is made up of 24 trillion cells, that make about 5000 trips through your body every day.
- Seven million new blood cells are being produced every second!
- Your body keeps up a temperature of 98.6 degrees.
- Your skin has over four million pores that act as a cooling system for the body.
- Your lungs give you all oxygen you need.

- Your digestive and metabolic systems are transforming the food you eat into blood, bone and cell structure.
- The human brain consists of more than 25 billion cells.
- There are over 75 trillion cells in your body.
- Within each tiny cell of your body there are thousands of components – chromosomes, genes, DNA, and so on.
- If you took all the DNA from all the genes of all your 75 trillion cells, it would fit into a box the size of an ice cube. But if all this DNA were unwound and joined together, the string would stretch from the earth to the sun and back more then 400 times – that's almost 80 billion miles!

Now I don't carry around all this information in my head, not even in my 25 billion or so brain cells. I don't understand a lot of it, but I know it's amazing. As you sit in this kirk, listening to this sermon – or even sleeping through it – your whole being is going through millions of intricate processes without you even being aware of it. It makes even the most sophisticated computer seem primitive. And you can listen to the words of the sermon, see the inside of the kirk, sense the atmosphere, and maybe even daydream all at the same time.

Human beings are miracles. A miracle doesn't cease to be a miracle just because it happens all the time.

Today, we baptise little Hannah Chirsty MacDonald. She is a little miracle in her own right. Hannah has her own unique blend of cells and genes and chromosomes. Her father, Iain, is not only a minister but a Hibs supporter, which would indicate, perhaps, that he didn't take on board the full consignment of brain cells ....

The Bible says that human beings have a glorious destiny. The Psalmist says that we are 'a little lower than the angels'. What a status!

The writer of the book of Genesis says that we are made in the image of God. What a wonderful thing to say. The Bible does not demean human beings.

That's why the Nazis, and the Japanese camp leaders, and the ethnic cleansers and the IRA and UDA terrorists are wrong – human beings are not cheap, or valueless, fit to be gassed, and stripped of gold fillings and minerals, worth a couple of pounds. We are fearfully and wonderfully made human beings.

Hugh MacDiarmid wrote a gorgeous little poem called 'The Bonnie Broukit Bairn':[1]

Mars is braw in crammasy,   crammasy = crimson
Venus in a green silk goun,
The auld mune shak's her gowden feathers,
Their starry talk's a wheen o' blethers,
Nane for thee a thochtie sparin',
Earth, thou bonnie broukit bairn!   broukit = neglected
– But greet, an' in your tears ye'll droun
The haill clanjamfrie!   clanjamfrie = collection

What MacDiarmid is saying with wonderfully economical and expressive language is that impressive though the whole solar system is, it is nothing compared to the glory of earth with its suffering humanity.

Or listen to Gerard Manley Hopkins:

The world is charged with the glory of God.
It will flame out, like shining from shook foil;
It gathers to a greatness, like the ooze of oil
Crushed. Why do men then now not reck his rod?
Generations have trod, have trod, have trod;
And all is seared with trade; bleared, smeared with toil;
And wears man's smudge and shares man's smell: the soil
Is bare now, nor can foot feel, being shod.

And for all this, nature is never spent;
There lives the dearest freshness deep down things;
And though the last lights off the black West went
Oh, morning, at the brow brink eastward, springs –
Because the Holy Ghost over the bent
World broods with warm breast and with ah! bright wings.[2]

We are of the earth, which is charged with the glory of God. We are made in the image of God, just a little lower than the angels. Each person is unique, valuable, with something of God in her or him. The stamp of the divine is hidden within each of us. It is where our potential for goodness and love lies. We are touched with bright wings, made for glory ...

and yet ... it's a flawed glory, isn't it?

We are a little lower than the angels, but sometimes no better than the beasts ... sometimes worse than that, because human beings do things that no animal would do.

James Froude said: 'Man is the only animal to whom the torture and death of his fellow creatures is amusing in itself.'

Mark Twain's verdict was: 'God made man at the end of the week when was tired.'

There is a flaw in our make up. The Bible calls it sin. St Paul says, *The things that I want to do, I can't ... and the things I don't want to do I find myself doing.*

We are made in the image of God, made for glory, made a little lower than the angels ... and yet as human beings we can act in the most appalling ways.

The truth is that inside all of us, there is, as Elisabeth Kubler-Ross says, a Mother Teresa and an Adolf Hitler. We can be both heroic and petty minded, capable of great love and great selfishness, all in the same week, all in the same minute.

Jesus Christ comes to us, bearing the love of God, embodying the love of God. He shows us what it is to be a truly human being – loving, open, vulnerable, caring. Not only that, by his death on the Cross, he provides a place of forgiveness.

He offers us freedom from our sin and weakness. And by his Resurrection, we are given the resources by which the Adolf Hitler in us can be diminished, the Mother Teresa in us allowed to grow and develop.

* * *

So, back to George Bush. 'Do you know who I am?' he asked. *If you don't know who you are, perhaps you should ask at the Information Desk.* The old lady spoke more than she knew.

We need to keep checking in at the Information Desk, to confirm who we are, and whose we are. That is at least part of what coming to church week by week is all about. We need to hear again and again that we are made in the image of God, that we are a little lower than the angels, that in our flawed yet glorious humanity we are forgiven and healed, and given the resources to help us to become what we truly are.

The sacraments are part of these resources for the journey, the process. Little Hannah is being checked in today.

'Do you know who I am?' she seems to ask us.

Yes, we know who she is: she is a little lower than the angels, with great things to do with her life. She is made in the image of God. She is a miracle of grace.

Hannah is accepted and loved before she can even articulate that knowledge. And some day, she will be asked the question: *But who do you say that I am?*

God give her the grace to say, with Peter, that flawed and glorious human being, *You are the Christ, Son of the Living God.*

---

1   Hugh MacDiarmid: 'The Bonnie Broukit Bairn' in Michael Grieve and Alexander Scott: *The Hugh MacDiarmid Anthology: Poems in Scots and English* (London: Routledge & Kegan Paul, 1977).
2   From Gerard Manley Hopkins: 'God's Grandeur' in *Oxford Book of Nineteenth Century English Verse* (Oxford: Oxford University Press).

CHAPTER 7

Blissward blown

IT used to be said of the town of Moose Jaw in the Saskatchewan prairies that one day the wind stopped, and everybody in the town fell down. I suppose that could sometimes be said of Orkney.

It reminds me of those matrons in the suburbs of Glasgow who would say 'my husband enjoys a wee refreshment', or, to make it even cosier, 'a wee refresh'. When you met the husbands you soon realised that most of the time they were seriously over-refreshed. Well, Orkney is a bit like that. Be on your guard when an Orcadian says it's a fresh day – it probably means that there's a 120 mile-an-hour gale blowing. Orkney is a truly fresh and refreshing place; but there can be days when you feel mightily over-refreshed, especially when you find yourself hanging on to buildings which are themselves hanging on to you.

In the Bible, the word for wind and spirit is the same. In Orkney, there's a lot of Spirit as well as a lot of wind. But we'll come back to that in a minute.

When I first came to Orkney, I asked a local man where he was going on holiday.

'Scotland,' he said.

My problem was that up till then I thought Orkney *was* in Scotland. I soon discovered differently – although, yes, Orkney actually *is* in Scotland, if you see what I mean. You don't? Oh, well, never mind.

Orkney is that group of islands beside Shetland which you usually find in a box, off the map of Scotland. Actually, there are more than 70 islands in Orkney, the largest of which is called the Mainland. Are you still with me? And while we're at it, it's wrong to talk about the

'Orkneys' – the word 'Orkney' *is* the plural. It's like calling Glasgow 'the Glasgows'. Are you coping with this information overload at this time on a Sunday morning?

When I first came here, well-meaning friends asked me: 'Isn't Orkney terribly far away?' Far away from *what*, though? This is like asking a man from Calcutta if he doesn't feel out of things. It all depends on your starting point.

Orkney is defined by two factors – geography and history. The geography you now know about. The history is fascinating. Walk through Kirkwall, past the Viking St Magnus Cathedral, and through streets like 'King Haakon Street' and Earl Sigurd Street' and 'Horda-land' and you start to wonder where you are. You're in that part of Norway which is forever Scotland. Is all this clear?

Orkney was colonised by the Vikings and run from Norway for five centuries. St Magnus Cathedral came under the jurisdiction of the Archbishop of Nidaros in Trondheim. Then, in 1471, as part of the political wheeling and dealing of the day, Orkney was transferred to Scotland. But although rulers and politicians can transfer land to another jurisdiction, you can't so easily transfer the hearts and minds and culture and identity of a people. Hence the schizophrenia. Hence going on holiday to Scotland when you are actually *in* Scotland. Orkney is Orkney is Orkney.

Orkney is also a place of warm hospitality, wide horizons and stunning seascapes. Its light in the summer time is exquisite and almost ethereal. It's easy to understand why people fall in love with the place and decide there and then to come and live here. Some adventurers come full of hopes, supported only by a sense of romance and a goat, seeking the simple life. But it's not as simple as that. Orkney may be beautiful, breathtakingly so, but it is a mistake to confuse it with the Garden of Eden. On a glorious, long June evening it may look as if it would be easy to live here – but working a croft in the dark winter days requires more than romance ....

People who don't know the Northern Isles sometimes imagine that life is rather rustic and primitive here. People from the south – that is, anywhere below John o' Groats – will ask tentatively about the ready availability of running water and electricity. One candidate for a teaching job recently asked whether there was any point in bringing his car – he wanted to know if there were roads in Orkney.

I have found Orkney to be a delightful mixture of simplicity and sophistication. It is a place of fierce independence and democratic inclination, with a strong sense of identity. It also has a strong sense of community. The interdependence that is a characteristic of farming communities is strengthened by living on an island and facing the vagaries of the weather together. The cultural life here is extraordinary.

The culture of Orkney can't be separated from its spirituality. When you look at the 5000 year old relics of Skara Brae and the tomb of Maeshow, or when you walk around the Ring of Brodgar, you can't help but be impressed by the sense of a long, spiritual journey. The power and beautiful awesomeness of the elements adds to the impact …

And then there is St Magnus Cathedral. Magnus was a martyr who died for the peace of Orkney, and his bones are interred here. There is something peaceable about the Cathedral, too. It has stood here for more than 800 years, a great shelter in the storms. The warmth of its pink and yellow sandstone has provided a welcome for many pilgrims down through the centuries. George Mackay Brown wrote a beautiful poem about the Cathedral, for the Society of the Friends of St Magnus. It is called 'The Kirk and the Ship'. Here it is:

The Master Mason said
'Sail to the Island of Eday
And quarry blocks of yellow stone.'
Others drove oxen to the Head of Holland
where sandstone is red.

The larks skein
About and about the April hill was thrown.

They did that work, the labouring Orkneymen.

Masons from Durham, strange speakers,
Squared the blocks, rough hewn.
They chiselled their marks, setting stone on stone,
And the Kirkwall villagers
Paused, and shook wondering heads, and went on.

And the kirk grew, like a lovely ship
Freighted with Psalm and ceremony, blissward blown.

Pillars soared up, red as fire or blood,
And in one they laid
Their martyr, Magnus: his breached bellchambered bone.

What a wonderful image – the Kirk as a ship. *Freighted with Psalm and ceremony, blissward blown.*

The ancient Christian faith, which this beautiful building represents, tells us that, at the end of the day, we are all blissward blown. Sometimes that is hard to believe. Sometimes it feels like hope against experience. But we are being drawn inexorably towards God.

Places are important. They shape the pilgrimage of our lives. In this series of broadcasts, I have talked about four places that have shaped my own life and faith – Cowdenbeath, Easterhouse, Iona and Orkney. They are very diverse places, but for me they have been places of epiphany, of revelation. And that revelation has come most of all through the lives of ordinary people.

When you travel in the Holy Land, it seems very odd to see signposts to places like Bethlehem and Nazareth. We have removed these biblical places from life by putting them into Gothic script and stained glass windows: but they are flesh and blood and brick-and-mortar places. Bethlehem was and is no great shakes as a town, but it was the cradle of hope.

For Bethlehem, read Cowdenbeath. Is that too fanciful? Or what about Easterhouse … or Iona … or Orkney … or Edinburgh … or Ayr … or wherever you have been in your life. They are all cradles, places of revelation – places where there are glimpses of God, or rumours of angels. When you look at the places you have been, you may even find traces of footprints, if you have eyes to see.

At the end of the day, though, all these special places are provisional, temporary. We are, sometimes despite the evidence of our lives, blissward blown.

For here we have no continuing city, but seek the city which is to come ....

CHAPTER 8

The Gunslinging Gambler
of Govan

IN MEMORIAM: GEORGE FIELDEN MACLEOD

I HAVE two texts. The first is from the 2 Timothy 4: 7 – *'I have fought the good fight: I have finished the race: I have kept the faith.'*

The second is from a piece of writing by George MacLeod. It's not from one of his great sermons or broadcasts, but a throwaway remark in a letter to Douglas Alexander ...

> *'I don't know why I went to Iona. God wanted it, and it was such a hell of a gamble that he could only find George MacLeod, who lost £40 one night at poker when he was waiting to be demobbed from the Agile and Suffering Highlanders.'*

* * *

I remember it well. I was in the refectory of Iona Abbey, when I was approached by a young and earnest member of staff, who was something of a classics scholar. He had been reading the Rule of the Iona Community – the little book which describes what it is that members of the Community commit themselves to when they join. He was troubled by the fact that the book was titled *Miles Christi*, which means 'Soldier of Christ'.

'How could George MacLeod, who is a pacifist, use such a military title?' he asked me. 'And why is it *miles*, singular, instead of *milites*, plural, when he is talking about a community?'

At that moment, as if on cue, the refectory door opened and in came the old thespian himself.

'There's George MacLeod – why don't you ask him?' I told the young man. And he did.

George thought for a moment, then he replied: 'I called it *Soldier of Christ* because we are engaged in a battle .... And I called it *Soldier*, singular, instead of *Soldiers*, plural, because when I made up the Rule I was the only Christian in the Community at the time!'

Exit ninety year old actor-manager on left, chuckling.

George MacLeod was what my aunty from Cowdenbeath would have called 'an awfy man'. And 'awfy' could be awfy awfy. He could be stubborn, imperious, insensitive, ruthless and manipulative. But George was 'awfy' in the other sense too – aweful and inspiring. Most people in this church today would have leapt out of the trenches with and for George – that's why we're here today. Not to put it too sentimentally, I loved him like I loved my own father.

* * *

What can one say about George MacLeod that hasn't been said already? I've written more than four hundred pages and used up many rain forests to try to capture the man – and still there's something elusive about him, thank God. We know all the cliches – a spiritual giant, one of the greatest Scotsmen of this century, and so on. Let's not bore George silly by repeating them.

The first occasion on which I encountered the man was when I was a young reporter with the *Edinburgh Evening News*. I was covering the General Assembly. When George started to speak, the words came pouring out in torrents, and I couldn't take him down in shorthand. Nor could the other reporters. We put our pencils down and listened, spellbound. He was that kind of orator.

The second time I met him was on Iona, when I went there as a student for the ministry. It so happened it was Community Week, when all the members of the Iona Community gather on the island. On the Wednesday pilgrimage, at the Marble Quarry, I listened, spellbound again, as George went through the history of the world – in about three minutes. Huge, sweeping, soaring generalisations. Whatever George MacLeod lacked, it wasn't confidence. In the middle of this oratorical *tour de force*, I heard a Community member behind me say in a stage whisper: 'How does he get away with it?' At that moment, I understood something of the relationship between George MacLeod and the Iona Community. How does he get away with it?

Let's not canonise George MacLeod, or imprison him in stained glass. Some people think that to meet this spiritual giant must have been the most ethereal and mystical of experiences. It was nothing of the kind. It was more like being *mugged*. You were safer on the streets of inner-city Glasgow at three o'clock in the morning than outside Iona Abbey in broad daylight when George MacLeod was on the rampage. What was even more lethal was to accept his invitation to whisky. That was to invite total brain meltdown, a taking leave of your senses, a consideration of life-changing possibilities which should never be seriously entertained in sobriety.

Most of us in this church have been spiritually mugged by George MacLeod, and we bear the marks in our life. And we're glad of it. That's why we're here. Because we have been wounded and lamed, and we wouldn't have it otherwise.

What can we say about him? He was a true soldier – a fighting man of immense bravery. You know, all his life he preferred the company of military men to pacifists. All his life he was a soldier looking for his lost regiment. All his life he was looking for battles to fight. He truly fought the good fight.

But above all else he was a *gambler*. And how the Church desperately needs gamblers today! He played cards for money in the trenches. He gambled his life in the Second Battle of Ypres, and came out alive but scarred. And when God needed a gambler for Iona, MacLeod was his man.

It's awesome today to stand in this pulpit where George MacLeod stood in May 1938 to bid farewell to the congregation he loved. When we see the restored abbey on Iona today, it all seems so right. We forget that in May 1938, with the storm clouds of war gathering over Europe, George MacLeod was taking an enormous gamble. He was leaving the security of the parish ministry, and of an assured career structure. When he was scratched, the man bled Moderator. It was in his blood. Yet he embarked on a wild goose scheme on a remote island, without ecclesiastical backing and without the necessary money.

'Could I have said no?' he asked the Govan congregation. 'Could I have said: "I am safe and happy in Govan and I am not going to take any risks whether half of Scotland goes pagan or not"? Or again, could I have gone on getting into the Govan pulpit and saying to our young people, "Christianity is an adventure; you must have to be prepared to take risks for Christ" and things like that (which I so often say), if in my heart I had known – and you had not known – that all these pointers had once come to me and I had skirted round them and had stayed on in a much safer billet than the one I am going to?'

Could he have said no? Well, yes, actually, he could have. He could have said no. But he didn't. And what an achievement that rebuilding was! And at what cost. To others. Just like *The Spire*, in William Golding's novel. What ruthless, frightening dedication it required! And the rebuilding was achieved at a cost to George himself. Despite his apparent confidence, every time he stood at Fionnphort on Mull and looked over to Iona, he had a knot in his stomach, just like he had when he went out to the Front in the First World War. I find that reassuring.

One way to understand the life of George MacLeod is to set it to music and see it as a Western in your own mind: with George in the role of the gambler. You always knew when George MacLeod was in town. The saloon doors burst open. George liked nothing better than a High Noon – he enjoyed a good fight the way some people enjoy bad health. He was no meek and mild pacifist – he was a *gun-slinging* pacifist. What he never fully understood, when he strode boldly down the street, was the number of sniper rifles trained on him from dilapidated buildings. Or maybe be did.

George MacLeod was a hero, a frontiersman, a mythic figure. Like Columba. This is supposed to be the age of the anti-hero, and heroes are very unfashionable today. But we need them at a very deep level. In one of the great books of this century, *The Denial of Death,* Ernest

Becker says that the urge to cosmic heroism is sacred and mysterious: and that we need 'new heroisms that are basically matters of belief and will, of dedication to a vision'. George MacLeod was a hero in that towering sense. That is quite different from being a celebrity – those hyped-up creatures of the media who are legends only in their own lunchtime.

He was also a perfect model of what Soren Kierkegaard called the 'Knight of Faith' – a member of an aristocracy of creative risk-takers for God. And it is impossible to give the gifts of the knight of faith without first being dubbed a knight by a Higher Majesty. That is the true aristocratic club to which George belonged, and the only one worth bothering about. It was the aristocracy of the pure in heart, those who single-mindedly serve God's purposes.

In America five years ago, George was asked by a minister how it was that he had managed to stay so single-minded all his life. When I relayed the question into George's ear, he replied: 'I have remained so single-minded all these years by being deaf!'

But there's more to it than that. In spite of his sophistication, George had a child-like faith. I am reminded of Karl Barth, author of *Church Dogmatics*. When asked by the media what the heart of his message was, the great professor thought for a minute then sang softly:

Jesus loves me this I know
For the Bible tells me so.

That child-like faith of George's was matched by a deep intuition, which allowed him to know things he couldn't fully explain. He didn't really understand science. He would quote Einstein repeatedly but he never read any of Einstein, never mind wrestled with his thinking. *How did he get away with it?* And yet he understood. How maddening!

Who can forget:

Invisible we see you, Christ beneath us.
With earthly eyes we see beneath us stones and dust and dross,
fit subjects for the analyst's table.

But with the eye of faith, we know you uphold.
In you all things consist and hang together;
The very atom is light energy, the grass is vibrant
the rocks pulsate.
All is in flux; turn but a stone and an angel moves.[1]

He had the lyrical heart of a Celtic poet. In his prayers and in his theology and in his life we have the fusion of the spiritual and the material, perhaps his greatest and most majestic gift to us.

Some people will feel that in a service centering on George MacLeod we should only be talking about ideas, and not the man himself, because that's what he surely would have done. I want to resist that notion. Because it is precisely in the flesh-and-blood man, in all his human frailties, that we have seen something of the glory of God. That is how God works. Truth is mediated through personality, incarnated, rooted, messy. All theology is, at the end of the day, biography, even when it's the biography of God. And, like you, I want to celebrate that life – particularly its heroism, its risk-taking, its flair, its passion, its romance, its excitement. It is a flawed life. The theological and psychological faultlines are there for all to see – but what a life!

And what of the future? It surely does not belong in imitating George MacLeod. God save us all from mini-MacLeods, or from George MacLeod fundamentalists! One of the reasons for writing George's biography was to make it impossible to be a MacLeod fundamentalist. George said so many different and contradictory things at different times that anyone trying to found a New Church of True Believers in George MacLeod deserves not just a dull life but a demented one as well.

What should we recommit our lives to, in gratitude for the life of George MacLeod? Can we work for a Church of Scotland which follows the Govan Gambler in taking risks, in going for broke? Can Scotland know that there truly is a Church in town? If we are going to go down the tubes, let us at least do it with style! The Kirk today is not short of decency and worthiness. But imagination and flair are not part of our strong suit.

Let us have a moratorium on 'Urgent Calls to the Kirk' and 'Urgent Calls to the Nation' and let us instead celebrate the gospel with laughter and tears and passion and style. Let us stop lecturing and hectoring the nation, and let's instead throw a party on the Mound and invite all of Scotland to join us.

You see, people cannot live by bread alone. We need a spiritual vision. But it will not come from an upright, moralising, tight-assed kirk, but one which is truly liberated. We are too sober by half, too prudent for our own good and the world's good. Let's get out of the kail-yard and the morass of *Sunday Post* moralising, and spend all that we've got. Let's abandon what Iain Crichton Smith calls 'survival without error' and go for double or quits. Let's lose our life in a gamble which may mean that we will truly find it. Or maybe not.

And while we're at it, let's have a truly ecumenical Church. George MacLeod, who through the sign of the rebuilt Iona Abbey has taught so many of us what it means to be ecumenical, is right again: the only ecumenical movement that is worth anything is one in which we are so close to one another that we can be rude to one another. Like George MacLeod, I want to be rude to my Roman Catholic brothers and sisters about the issue of inter-communion. I want to say to you in all honesty: 'Despite all your theological sophistication, I don't think you fully realise what you are doing to us all.' If I hear any more hand-wringing talk about the unavoidable pain of our unhappy divisions, I think I will scream. In fact, I want to scream that pain. In a day when there are so many exciting alternative religious options for people, our historic Christian divisions feel more and more like archaic and self-indulgent obstacles.

Here's something that we Christians should give up for Lent and beyond: all talk of Christianity as a religion of reconciliation. As we sit back-to-back at separate tables, we are a laughing-stock, and not all the sophisticated talk in the world about the non-negotiable nature of truth can cover our nakedness. Any little kid in Govan can see that at this stage the Christian emperor has no clothes.

Having been involved in a number of ecumenical ventures, I believe that George MacLeod is right: as well as polite ecumenical conversations, we need the liturgical and street theatre of outright shame. And I hope that our Roman Catholic sisters and brothers will feel free to be rude to those of us who are Protestant, about our failings: for instance, about the lack of mystery and poetry of our worship, where so much of our liturgy has all the grace and beauty of a local government memo or a Department of Social Services pamphlet about heating allowances for pensioners.

Yes, we need an ecumenical movement which faces the issues and takes risks. Iona Abbey, which is home for all denominations, is a place for such risk-taking. Wouldn't it be marvellous if, in the year 2000, the Pope came to Iona Abbey and marked two millennia of Christianity by inaugurating a new era of Christian freedom and adventure: celebrated by offering the bread and wine to all believers! People would then know that there was a real Church in town: an emperor with some clothes – even if they're from the Oxfam shop. And perhaps even nail-prints in his hands.

And who knows, perhaps Christianity itself will undergo a transformation equivalent to the overcoming of the split between Jew and Gentile. The words of George MacLeod's grandfather, the great Norman, are pertinent here:

> *Where is the germ of the church of the future? .... Neither Calvinism, nor Presbyterianism, nor Thirty Nine Articles, nor High Churchism nor Low Churchism, nor any existing organisation can be the church of the future! May God give us patience to wait!*

We need to be inspired by George MacLeod, but also to transcend his limitations. Can we commit ourselves to work for a Church and society in which the qualities of the feminine are honoured as much as those of the masculine, the intuitive as much as the rational? If our religious and political institutions are to be transformed, we need to start right here.

We live in very exciting times. It is an exciting time to be the Church. Did you think you would live to see the day when the Berlin Wall would come down? When Nelson Mandela would be released from prison? When the Communist Party would be legal in Britain and banned in Russia?

Can we have a Church which rejoices at the overthrow of tyrannical communism in Russia and Eastern Europe and at the same time asks tough questions about how democratic and accountable our own institutions are? Peace and disarmament and justice are now on the world's agenda in a way which George MacLeod could only have dreamed of – and did dream of – a few years ago. And the challenge to all of us now is to move from slogans to specifics, from knee-jerk responses to creative solutions.

Can we have a Church in Scotland – and of course beyond Scotland – which will work passionately and imaginatively for peace and disarmament, and for justice for the world's poor and hungry? A Church which forces these matters on to the political agenda, and ensures that elections aren't simply about our own precious standard of living?

When George MacLeod was awarded the Templeton International Prize in 1989, he wasn't interested in the glory. He wanted the money. And he wanted it to give it all away to the causes most dear to his heart: peace, and the ending of poverty.

One thing George would never forgive me for would be if I were to allow more than 1000 people to leave this church without being asked to sign up for a new crusade. So as you leave there will be a petition. We can do no less for George. It simply calls on all the political parties of this country to ensure that the issues of peace and justice for the world's poor are made central to the debate at the next general election. Perhaps at the next election, as well as the West Lothian Question, we can have the George MacLeod Question: How can the 'peace dividend' which comes from the ending of the Cold War be invested in the future of the poor of the world?

I began with the old actor-manager in the refectory of Iona Abbey. I close with the same man in the new reconciliation centre at Iona which bears his name. When we first took George into the new MacLeod Centre, a few days before the official opening in 1988, the first thing he did was to repeat the Lord's Prayer in a loud voice. We were touched by this display of piety. Then the old rogue turned, and said with a twinkle: 'I was only testing the acoustics!'

After the opening ceremony, George and Leah Tutu and some of us linked arms and almost danced into the Centre. George, without his sticks, was almost airborne. And as we all sang the South African spiritual 'We are marching in the light of God', George's voice sounded uncannily like that of a child. 'Marching in the Light of God' is what George's life has been about. Let us march in his company, inspired by him without being commanded by him. Let us dance along with him, and sing the Resurrection songs with childlike voices.

Let us fight the good fight. Let us finish the race. Let us keep the faith; remembering that

> *those who wait on the Lord shall renew their strength:*
> *they shall mount up on wings as eagles:*
> *they shall run and not be weary:*
> *they shall walk and not faint.*

Or to put it in the words of this new hymn:

> *Think not to weary*
> *or lay your great commission down;*
> *nor crave approval*
> *nor fear the critic's frown.*
> *Prevail through tears, love with laughter,*
> *risk all, then hereafter*
> *receive from Christ your crown.*[2]

George MacLeod, *Miles Christi*, Soldier of Christ: you have fought the good fight. You have finished the race. You have kept the faith.

George MacLeod, Gambler of Govan: when will we see your likes again?

---

1 George F MacLeod: *The Whole Earth Shall Cry Glory – Iona Prayers* (Glasgow: Wild Goose Publications, 1985).
2 From a hymn written for the occasion by John L Bell and Graham Maule.

MacLeod: The Seer

*That half-cocked eye searches
me in quizzical mode,
defying, defying.
Its look is humorous,
with a hint of murder. (The kind
which pacifists can only dream of.)*

*You would write my life,
would you?
Of course you can try*

to cross into no man's land but
the trench is deep and
the corpses are stinking on singing wires and
there are unexploded mines,
mind you.
Of course you can try
to make me remember
(of course you can try)

says the eye, winking
and glinting friendly furious
in the fading sunlight.
That private public eye has seen
into the ghostly past – don't
linger there for Christ's sake –
and on into the present, tense:
has dwelt on horrors and trembling moved to vision
a new thing, desperate.
No eye for an eye is this
which has seen the glory
of the coming of the Lord,
has learned to fear that terrible swift sword
which stabs awake at night.

And when the ferryman comes with ropes of pain
and blocks and tackle –
not still the red boat of MacBrayne? –
the hooded far-seeing jewel stays open,
half, watchful and controlling.
A hundred years in thy sight
are but yesterday when it is gone, O Lord
MacLeod of the ever-watchful pupil,
who neither slumbers nor sleeps.

Ron Ferguson

CHAPTER 9

Breath and Bread

JANUARY. It's cold. The winds outside St Magnus Cathedral – this great medieval shelter – are strong. The days are dark and long. Christmas is but a memory. The bills are coming in.

There's a lot to be said for hibernation, isn't there – going to bed until the Spring comes again.

There used to be a saying in Fife when I was a boy:

If at first you don't succeed,
Pull the blankets ower yer heid.

Do you know that feeling?

We've experienced the mountaintop of Christmas, and the next one won't be till Easter, Springtime: till the green shoots come up again. How are we to live in the valleys? What resources do we need?

I'm drawn back time and again to these marvellous words of Gerard Manley Hopkins:

Thou mastering me
God! Giver of breath and bread.

Breath and bread: that's what we need. In a sense, that's *all* we need. It may not be all we want, but God isn't Santa Claus. This is for real: for the cold days, for the dark days, in the valleys.

Breath is fundamental to our life. Without that breath in our lungs, we literally cannot live.

In the Old Testament, the word for 'breath' in the Hebrew is *Ruach*. It also means 'spirit'.

In the New Testament, the Greek word for 'breath' is *pneuma*. It also means 'spirit'.

So in the Bible, the words for 'breath' and 'spirit' are virtually interchangeable. Without this Godbreathed spirit, we are not human beings. This notion goes right back to the ancient story of Creation.

> *In the day that the Lord God made the earth and the heavens, when no plant of the field was yet in the earth ... then the Lord God formed man from the dust of the ground, and breathed into his nostrils the breath of life; and man became a living being.*
>
> Genesis 2: 4-7

And when the breath is withdrawn? Earth to earth ... ashes to ashes ... dust to dust. As the Psalmist puts it:

> *When thou hidest thy face, they are dismayed;*
> *when thou takest away their breath, they die*
> *and return to their dust.*
> *When thou sendest forth thy spirit,*
> *they are created;*
> *and thou renewest the face of the ground.*
>
> Psalm 104: 29, 30

What about bread? It's just as basic as breath. And God provides it, too.

When the Israelite slaves made their escape to freedom in the Exodus from Egypt, they rightly wondered where their next meal would come from. God promised them that he would rain down bread from heaven.

It came in the form of *manna*.

Manna in the Hebrew simply means, 'What is it?'

Every mother knows what manna is. You know, you put down lovely meals for the kids, and they moan, 'What is it?'

The Hebrews kept complaining to Moses, 'Not manna again?' They had manna fried, manna poached, manna scrambled, manna raw. And it still tasted like 'What is it?' They couldn't even have manna and chips. There was no wee chip van out there in the wilderness selling manna suppers and a bottle of Irn Bru®. It was just ... well ... manna.

The people got fed up with it. And they remembered the good old days.

And the people of Israel also wept again, and said, 'O that we had meat to eat! We remember the fish we ate in Egypt for nothing, the cucumbers, the melons, the leeks the onions and the garlic; but now our strength is dried up, and there is nothing at all but this manna to look at'.

Oh dear ... this SAGA tour hadn't turned out to be as good as they thought, and they wanted their money back please.

But wait a minute. Weren't their memories just a tad selective? Cucumbers and watermelons? Were the good old days really that good? What about making bricks out of straw, and being lashed by the Pharaoh's men?

It seems that faced with yet more 'manna, glorious manna', the people of Israel would have exchanged their political and religious freedom for an Egyptian carry-out. We're not talking heroism here.

But what about the people of the world who have no bread: those who can't remember the cucumbers and watermelons, and would love to get their hands on just a little manna? What are the children of Somalia to make of all this 'bread of heaven' stuff?

In the Exodus story, God tells the people in the wilderness that there will be enough for everybody – but if they try to hoard it, it will go bad. And that's exactly what happens.

Today, there's enough bread around to feed the world, but we've got it stored in our freezers. And it's going bad on us, spiritually, to the destruction of our souls and ultimately our bodies. We have more than our share of bread, and we refuse to release our grip. We even surround ourselves with barbed wire and floodlights to protect our extra goodies, and we don't even realise that we're in a prison of our own making ...

How can we be persuaded to release our grip on the extra bread we're hoarding? We cannot live by bread alone. The bread goes bad on us if we have no spiritual vision. And this brings us back to breath. Without the God-breathed spirit, we are dead men and women.

In order to be card-carrying members of the human race, we need bread-material and breath-spirit. But spirituality is not a matter of deep breathing through alternate nostrils, or getting into the lotus position on top of a greasy pole: our spirituality, says Jesus, is seen in what we do with our bread.

Where there is no vision, the people perish ...

*   *   *

'Where are we to get bread enough in the desert to feed so great a crowd?' the disciples asked Jesus as the five thousand pressed in against them. One of the sure signs of the kingdom of God is that bread is multiplied and passed from hand to hand.

In the Scottish Presbyterian tradition, at Holy Communion, we pass the bread from one to another: this broken bread. 'This is my body, broken for you ....' The symbolism of this passing from hand to hand is important.

I can't receive the Bread of Life unless my neighbour passes it to me. And my neighbour can't receive it unless I pass it to her.

If I keep it to myself, my neighbour starves spiritually. If I hoard the loaves in my freezer, my neighbour dies physically. What I don't notice is that I die spiritually in the process.

One of the great heresies of today is that there is no such thing as society. That kind of statement can only be made from behind the barbed wire of the spiritual death camp, that prison of our own making. If we live in a society in which the neighbour is there to be ripped off or abandoned in the wilderness, our bread becomes for us what the Bible calls 'the bread of bitterness'.

Christ is in the neighbour, and Christ is in the bread. He is at the heart of the sacrament of the universe.

I am the Bread of Life. He who comes to me shall not hunger, and he who believes in me shall never thirst .... Your fathers ate manna in the wilderness and they died. This is the bread that comes down from heaven, that a man may eat of it and not die.

The manna of the wilderness has become the Bread of Life. Angus Peter Campbell talks of it in this way in his collection of poems, *The Greatest Gift:*

I go outside
and the desert is a white frost,
thin flakes of frost covering the hot sand:
manna? the people ask, and I also wonder.
What is this thin frost that covers the desert sand.

I step out
past Moses, beyond Joshua, into the promised land:
thin flakes of frost covering the hot hot sand – manna?
What is this
that slouches towards Bethlehem, this new Jerusalem
this King on a donkey, these crosses, this fire,
this new covenant, this new frost, this new delivery,
this fresh Exodus.

What is the meaning
of this vast desert morning
and a million of our people, the delivered ones,
asking what it is,
this white thing that looks like coriander seed and tastes like honey.

The writer concludes the poem/meditation:

I went to church last Sunday
and I heard the minister preaching:
'I am the bread of life', he said,
'and he who comes to me will never go hungry',
and I saying now, after the Exodus and the cross,
'I believe': this white thing is manna,
this thin frost is bread, this thing is atonement,
white frost, coriander seed, honey sweet, a life.[1]

As I look forward in these January days to the coming green and gold of the fertile fields of Orkney, set beside the ancient standing stones of history and the silent but eloquent walls of Skara Brae, I am reminded of the words of Alice Meynell:

Lurking in the cornfield
Furtive in the vine
Lonely unconsecrated host.

It's January. The wind is still blowing around the ancient walls of this Cathedral. And the days are long and dark. And the bills are still coming in, damn them.

But the flags of a new dawn are appearing. We are beginning to understand that the material is but the cradle of the spiritual.

And he promises – this strange, winter Christ who is born to die and rise again when the green blade rises – he promises: *blessed is the one who shall eat bread in the kingdom of God.*

---

1   Angus Peter Campbell: 'Manna, meaning what is it?' in *The Greatest Gift* (London: Fountain Publishing, 1992).

CHAPTER 10

Breasts and Bread

Is this not the fast that I have chosen: to let the oppressed go free and to share your bread with the hungry?

Isaiah 58: 6

But Jesus turning to them said: 'Daughters of Jerusalem, do not weep for me, but weep for yourselves and for your children. For indeed the days are coming when they will say, 'Blessed are the barren, the wombs that never bore, and the breasts which never nursed.'

Luke 23: 28

THIS morning I want to preach about breasts.

Not many sermons in St Magnus Cathedral have begun in this precise manner, but we live in extraordinary, almost apocalyptic times.

The most famous breasts this week are those attached to the personage known as the Duchess of York, pictured in close negotiations with her financial adviser.[1] Now I don't really need to tell you this, unless you've been living in a cave out by Yesnaby. The semi-royal mammaries have been on public view, thanks to the good and public-spirited offices of the Scottish paper, the *Daily Record*.

It may seem more than a little vulgar to refer to such matters from the pulpit, but the fact that the precious royal nipples have forced such lesser things as wars and pestilence off the newspaper front pages and television screens for a whole week tells us something about the nature of the times in which we live.

The circulation of the tabloids dramatically increased this week. In fact, on the first day of sale, enterprising news vendors were selling each copy for a pound. It seems as if most of the nation was slavering over these pictures, or being indignant about them, or even both. I suspect most of us in this congregation couldn't resist a peek at the photos of this highly unusual poolside discussion about the Dow Jones.

The photographer who crawled through the undergrowth to get the snaps is now apparently more than one million pounds richer. It was a good day at the office for this daring entrepreneur, this fine example of the enterprise culture which is being held up to us approvingly every day.

Let me tell you about another pair of breasts. They belong to another woman in her thirties, but they will never be in *Playboy* or *Paris Match*. No photographer will get one million pounds for photographing them. They are not objects of sexual stimulation. You see, the breasts themselves are shrivelled and empty. Because the woman lives in Somalia.

Daughters of Jerusalem, do not weep for me but weep for yourselves and for your children. For indeed the days are coming in which they will say: 'Blessed are the barren, the wombs that never bore, and the breasts which never nursed.'

What pitiful pictures we are seeing, of wretched humanity. Twenty million people at risk of death in Africa! We've known about this holocaust for some time. Men, women and children. One woman died when out foraging for bread; her two waiting, starving children were later found dead. They had been reduced to eating sand. Where is our sense of pity?

In the light of all this, there is something more than distasteful about the attention overkill for royal hangers-on cavorting around the playgrounds of Europe at our expense. That is the real obscenity. There are certainly some members of the royal entourage who should get their UB40s in the post. As I search the scriptures I cannot find anything which justifies that kind of pampered and expensive lifestyle while children die in abject misery.

* * *

This kind of situation is not new in human history. At the time of the prophet Isaiah, the poor were being miserably treated while the rich danced. And the same people who were robbing the poor and grinding their faces in the dust were going along to the temple in Jerusalem to go through all the religious rituals. And they were quite pleased with themselves.

Isaiah, as he looks around at what is happening, can contain himself no longer. He is burning with the word of God (58: 1-7):

Cry aloud and spare not.
Lift up your voice like a trumpet.
Tell my people their transgression,
and the house of Jacob their sins.

In fact, in the day of your fast you find pleasure,
And exploit all your labourers.
Indeed you fast for strife and debate,
and to strike with the fist of wickedness.
Is it a fast that I have chosen,
a day for a man to afflict his soul?
Is it to bow down his head like a bulrush,
and to spread out sackcloth and ashes?
Would you call this a fast
and an acceptable day to the Lord?

Is not this the fast that I have chosen:
to loose the bonds of wickedness,
to undo the heavy burdens,
to let the oppressed go free,
and that you break every yoke?
Is it not to share your bread with the hungry,
and that you bring to your house the poor who are cast out;
when you see the naked that you cover him,
and not hide yourself from your own flesh?

66

We're living in days of bread and circuses. The circuses are getting more tawdry by the minute, and our bread is stamped firmly with the words 'hands off'.

But what are we to do? It's all so overwhelming, is it not?

The first thing we can do is to give money – the need is immediate.

The political solutions have to come from the politicians. But we in the Church should be helping to create a groundswell for justice for the poor of the world. We should say – and mean it – that

- we want fair trading for the poor who are exploited;
- we are prepared to reduce our lifestyle expectations, so that the poor may be lifted out of starvation;
- our country should no longer bankroll civil wars, and supply arms to dictators throughout the world;
- we do not want to shelter under the defence of obscenely expensive Trident missiles while the poor of the world die for want of bread and medicine.

And we need to look at our priorities, to see how they match the priorities of the kingdom of God, to remember that the fast the Lord requires of us is to loose the bonds of wickedness and to share our bread with the hungry.

And Isaiah says that when the world learns to do this, there will be a change (58: 8, 9).

Then your light shall break forth like the morning,
your healing shall spring forth speedily,
and your righteousness shall go before you;
The glory of the lord shall be your rearguard.
Then you shall call, and the Lord will answer;
You shall cry, and he will say:
Here I am.

In the Western neck of the woods we have become jaded, sated. The Duchess of York's breasts have proved to be worth several million pounds each to a number of people. Today's vanity, and the pressures of fashion, have made millions for the makers of silicone, while the lamentations of the emaciated young women with the dry and shrivelled breasts, weeping for their children, are ignored by a rich world with its hearing-aid firmly switched to the 'off' position.

Bread is at the heart of our faith. *This is the body of Christ, broken for you.*

Whatever we do to the least of these, we do to him. To pass the bread to our neighbour in Somalia or Bosnia or elsewhere is to touch the garment of the living Christ.

CHAPTER 11

Tam and Bess

Jesus said to him: 'Thomas, because you have seen me, you have believed. Blessed are those who have not seen, and yet have believed.'
John 20: 29

OUR ginger cat was a stray, a refugee from a farm in Evie, Orkney. The farmer's wife told us how the cat had appeared one day and confidently declined the invitation to go away; they already had too many cats, and were looking for a good home. She was, said the wife, a very affectionate little creature.

When we got the cat – by this time dubbed Evie – back home, we wondered if, being female and a stray, she might be expecting a series of happy little events. So, we took her to the vet who told us, after an examination, that not only was she not pregnant, she was actually a he. So she, now he, became Tam.

Tam was utterly unaffected by this identity crisis. In fact, he seems utterly unaffected by anything. He walks through the world with complete confidence. When he lies on the bed, or sits on your lap, you can hear him purring away, like a Rolls Royce, full of contentment. He has the happy knack of making himself very comfortable.

Wee Tam's life is secure and sunny, literally. He sits in the sun in at the kitchen window ... his own private little conservatory. He doesn't doubt for a minute that his dinner will be there. Tam has no such doubts or fears. He strolls imperiously, and sometimes disdainfully, through his world, knowing that all will be well, and all manner of things will be well. While I, like most clergy, rush around Saving the World, the manse cat sleeps unproductively and serenely in the sun. The

Protestant Work Ethic has maddeningly passed him by. His world is secure, and does not need to be questioned. No Doubting Tam is he …

Not like our dog, Bess, a collie-cross. She – yes, definitely *she* – likes to remind you that it's time for certain things, like walkies. Just in case you've forgotten. She sticks her face in front of you, and fixes you with brown, soulful eyes. She needs reassurance about the order of things.

You see, Bess's experience of life has been different. She was abandoned, after having had several beatings. When we first got her, she would back away from any adult who approached, and would cross the road if she saw a man coming towards her. Nothing is secure. She always fears the worst.

Adults are more complex than cats or dogs, but our early experiences help shape how we see the world. I wonder what childhood experiences the disciple we know as Thomas had? His name is hardly mentioned now without the epithet 'Doubting', as if that were his defining characteristic.

The meagre evidence we have about Thomas suggests that he was loyal, determined, and a pessimist. He would always see the worst. For instance, when Jesus tells his friends that Lazarus is dead, Thomas says: 'Let us also go, that we may die with him.' Is that reaction not just a little bit over the top?

Thomas is more like Bess the Dog than Tam the Cat. We don't know anything about his early experiences, but evidently he is the kind of character who expects the worst. He is a member of that club whose name is legion – the religious pessimists. My mother used to have a cautionary saying, 'There's aye a something'. The trouble with that kind of view is that you can waste a fair bit of your life examining the teeth of gift horses.

- The optimist says: 'Every cloud has a silver lining.'
- The pessimist says: 'Every silver lining has a cloud.'
- The optimist says: 'Isn't it marvellous to see the longer light in Orkney!'
- The pessimist says: 'The nights will soon be drawing in.'

- The optimist says: 'What a lovely day!'
- The pessimist says: 'Aye, we'll pay for it.'
- Tam the Cat says: 'Now that I've spent the day sunning myself, I'll go and get my dinner.'
- Bess the Dog says: 'I wonder if I'll get any dinner today?'

It's not enough to say that optimists are better than pessimists. Pessimists can often be much more realistic about life: and ever-cheery optimists can sometimes be a pain in the neck.

Thomas has probably had disappointments in the past. Maybe expectations have been built up, and his hopes have been dashed, again and again. This time, he's not going to be carried away. Big Tam is the kind of man who expects the worst, and if good unexpectedly happens – well, that's a bonus. Lots of people live their lives on this basis. Aberdeen supporters, for instance. They usually predict relegation every year, while fantasising in secret that their team will win the European Cup.

Now, I am well aware that I have been building up a picture of Thomas on the basis of a few clues. Writers and preachers do this all the time – it makes life much more fun. It could be that Thomas was actually the cheeriest man in the pub, freely and volubly predicting that Nazareth Primrose would hammer Jerusalem Rangers in the next round of the cup. As a Cowdenbeath supporter, and therefore one who knows more about ridiculous fantasy than most, I would like to think it were true, but, like Thomas, I doubt it.

One thing for sure. Thomas is not going to believe all this stuff about the Resurrection of Jesus until he has 100 per cent proof. The story in John's Gospel tells us that the first time Jesus came to the disciples after the Resurrection, Thomas wasn't present. Why not? The Gospel doesn't tell us, but I've a hunch that he might have been on his own, facing his own hurt and grief and disappointment. You see, despite their public 'front', most pessimists secretly hope that something good will happen, even if they have predicted that it wouldn't. While there is a certain grim satisfaction in being proved right – remember that plaintive tombstone epitaph, 'I kept telling you I was ill' – pessimists have to hide their own private devastation while maintaining a cool 'I told you so' facade. Aye, it's a hard life.

So when Thomas finally rejoins the others, having done his weeping alone, they tell him: 'We have seen the Lord.' But Thomas, being the good pessimist and realist that he is, says, 'Aye, that'll be right. I'll believe it when I see it'. Then he lays down his conditions for belief: 'Unless I see in his hands the print of the nails, and put my finger into the print of the nails, and put my hands into his side, I will not believe.'

So there.

I have a lot of sympathy for Thomas. Why should he believe? After all, Resurrections aren't simply everyday tales of farming folk. If someone were to claim a rising from the dead in Orkney today, would *you* believe it?

No. Resurrections are not ordinary events. The *Orcadian* doesn't report a couple of risings from the dead every week. You don't see it in the personal column – 'I wish to thank those who gave me a glass of Highland Park after I rose from the dead in Kirkwall last week.'

So Thomas, the patron saint of doubters, asks for proof. That's hardly unreasonable, from a hurting man who would secretly like to live out his wildest dreams. He's not prepared to suspend his critical faculties just because the disciples are in a minor frenzy. He's going to keep his feet firmly on the ground.

But Jesus knows Thomas. He loves him. Suddenly, the Lord is in the midst of the disciples. It's all very mysterious. Closed doors … what kind of body? Paul talks about a spiritual body – a contradiction in terms. Both St Paul and St John are trying to use language to describe things which are literally beyond language.

Jesus knows what Thomas needs. He says to Thomas: *Reach your fingers here, and look at my hands; and reach your hand here, and put it into my side. Do not be unbelieving, but believing.*

Thomas doesn't need to touch Jesus. He can see for himself. He doesn't need anything else to convince him. He has all the proof he needs.

My lord and my God, he says.

Now that Doubting Thomas is convinced, he doesn't hold back. He goes the whole way. *My lord and my God.* He knows that he isn't going to be let down this time. He can let go. He doesn't have to be a pessimist any more. He can simply be a happy realist – someone with good grounds for hope.

Christian faith doesn't ask us to chose between optimism and pessimism. It says here is realism – a faith that knows dark times, but will last beyond death.

Jesus says to him: *Thomas, because you have seen me, you have believed. Blessed are those who have not seen, and yet have believed.*

* * *

I find this story very encouraging. It says to us that Jesus accepts us as we are, doubts and all. It says it's all right to come with our doubts and dark fears. It says that the Church, like the disciples, is for assured people and doubters, righteous people and sinners, people who know what they believe and people who hang on to faith by their fingernails.

Some people have their faith sussed out: others feel out of things. Most of us humans have times of faith and times of doubt.

Jesus says: Peace. Come with me on a journey of discovery. He also says you don't have to see to believe. This is a beautiful story, a story of hope – for all kinds of people.

When I go back to the manse today, Tam the Cat may be sitting in the sun at the window, full of assurance and confidence. Bess the Dog may have to check first that there are no strangers with me.

And I will see them, and think of Doubting Tam from Palestine, and Jesus, and nail prints, and faith. And I will be glad. Glad that it takes all kinds to make a world. Glad that it takes all kinds of weird and truly wonderful travelling people to make a Church.

CHAPTER 12

100,000 Lemmings
can't be wrong

And those who went before and those who followed cried out, saying: 'Hosanna! Blessed is he who comes in the name of the Lord!'

Mark 11: 9

And Pilate said to them: 'Why, what evil has he done?' But they shouted all the more, 'Crucify him!'

Mark 15: 14

THE thrill of being in a big crowd is unforgettable. To stand, for instance, on the terracing at Hampden or Murrayfield and to sing with the crowd is quite special.

My earliest memory of being in a big crowd was at a football match in my home town of Cowdenbeath. There were 25,586 people in the ground for the visit of Glasgow Rangers. It was a Wednesday afternoon and I should have been at school, but I was at the game, perched on my dad's shoulders.

The significance of the occasion was that it was the quarter final of the Scottish League Cup. In the first leg Cowdenbeath had gone to Ibrox and beaten Rangers 3-2. They had gone into the lions' den and attacked the lions.

Rangers, humiliated by that defeat at Ibrox, were going to sort out the Second Division upstarts. So, more than twice the population of Cowdenbeath was packed into Central Park. I can still remember the atmosphere in the crowd. It was electric.

The game started, with all the Cowdenbeath supporters feeling very nervous, waiting for the first goal. It came in six minutes – but it was a goal for Cowdenbeath! This was not in the script. The excitement was tremendous. The part-time miners were now 4-2 ahead on aggregate!

Then Rangers equalised. Ah, yes, the goal avalanche would start now. Cowdenbeath defended desperately.

With only 13 seconds to go, big George Young, the Rangers and Scotland captain, punted the ball forward. The weary Cowdenbeath defence hesitated, and Johnny Rutherford nipped in to score. It was 4-4 on aggregate.

Absolute deflation ....

Extra time – Rangers scored. Cowdenbeath 4, Rangers 5. The Cowdenbeath supporters were desolate. I saw grown men, miners, weeping. They had travelled the whole gamut of emotions – from nervousness, to fear, to hope, to elation, to despair. Even now, I can conjure up the feelings.

*   *   *

What is just as impressive is when a huge crowd falls silent.

Another memory. As a young journalist, I stood with silent crowds at the pithead of the Lindsay colliery in Kelty as bodies of dead miners were brought to the surface. I cannot forget the anxious women, their pale, strained faces framed by headscarves, waiting for news of their menfolk. Nor can I forget the quiet dignity of the crowds of miners in their best suits, walking silently behind the coffins, and standing in complete silence at the empty graves, tears rolling down the strong faces.

But crowds can also be very dangerous, very frightening.

Think about Nazi Germany. The thousands who crowded into the Nurnberg stadium felt exhilarated as they sang the nationalist songs. Buoyed up, these clerks and civil servants and housewives shared in the hellish bloodlust.

Stuart McWilliam, a Church of Scotland minister, was at a Palm Sunday service in 1938 in the little German University town of Marburg. He remembered:

I heard that day a sermon which I have never forgotten. At that time I had been only a short time in Germany and by mistake I went to a Nazi church .... The preacher began by describing the entry of Christ into Jerusalem and from it he drew a parallel with the entry of Hitler into Vienna which had taken place fairly recently. While comparatively few people hailed the entry of Christ into Jerusalem, that of Hitler into Vienna was triumphantly acclaimed by 80 million Germans. He left one in no doubt as to which event he regarded as the more significant ....

Crowds can be manipulated to do bestial things. People end up doing things in a crowd they would never dream of doing as individuals. There's something about the security and anonymity of a crowd that can make you feel everything's all right. Yet it might be all wrong. A piece of graffiti on a cliff in Palestine says it with telling irony – *100,000 lemmings can't be wrong!*

Crowds can also be very fickle. The mood can change very quickly. Things may start in good humour, and end up in a murderous rage. The same people can turn from dignity and nobility to a frenzied search for a victim, any victim.

Jesus, on that first Palm Sunday, knew that. He knew what was in people. He was under no illusions.

Let's think about the crowd on that first Palm Sunday, shouting 'Hosanna' as Jesus begins his lonely journey into Jerusalem.

What kind of people are there? All kinds. There is great excitement in the air because the Passover is beckoning.

Over there is a wealthy merchant, someone who sells pigeons in the temple. His 'Hosanna' is a bit half-hearted; he is wondering whether this Jesus will be good for business. He has a surprise coming.

Down here is a man with dark, wild eyes. He looks a bit suspicious, his hand always going into his robe. He seems to be watching rather than participating. He is a Zealot, one of a band of assassins called the *siccarii*. It is a dagger which he keeps fondling. He hates Rome, and is wondering whether this Jesus is going to overthrow the Romans with violence. A friend of his, Barrabas, was caught by the Romans only last week, and is presently in prison under sentence of death.

Over there, a man runs away from the crowd, towards the city. He is an informer, paid by Caiaphas the High Priest. He is going to report that Jesus of Nazareth is on his way.

Down here, a man gets ready to set up his food and drink stall. Wherever there's a crowd, he's on the lookout for business.

Then there are the ones full of devotion. They've heard Jesus preach, and they know he's got something special. They shout 'Hosanna' very enthusiastically. Someone holds up a child, hoping the Messiah will bless the baby.

Also in the crowd are people who feel the tension, who sense that Jesus is going to his death. They don't want to miss the drama. They are the kind of people who today stop their cars to go and look at a car crash. They are the voyeurs of tragedy.

Then there are the flavour-of-the-month people who want to be fashionable. They want to back a winner, and for the moment Jesus of Nazareth looks like a winner. He's the talk of the town. It's all happening around him. There's a buzz, and these people want to say 'I was there'.

There are the disciples, full of hope and expectation. Their moment has arrived. Jesus has come to claim his kingdom at last, and they will be top dogs. They have been looking forward to this tryst with destiny for a long, long time.

In the middle of the crowd is Jesus of Nazareth. He knows crowds can be exhilarating and inspiring – and also fickle and dangerous. He knows that his supporters will probably turn against him, or desert him. Yes, he knows that. But he is steadfast.

And so he moves towards Jerusalem, on a donkey – the symbol of peace, of lowliness. The palm branches wave. The shouts of 'Hosanna' go up.

Ride on, ride on in majesty!
The winged squadrons of the sky
Look down with sad and wondering eyes
to see the approaching sacrifice.

Hymn 234, Church Hymnary (third edition)

His journey takes him through the upper room – 'this is my body' – to Gethsemane, where his disciples fall asleep. Then on to the temple. He throws out the money lenders. That's some supporters he's lost already.

There are people waiting for him. The high priest and his men. The informers have done their work. Jesus is silent before his accusers. The Zealots, who thought he might be a revolutionary, melt away into the night.

He is taken away. The people who thought he was the man of the moment vanish into the night. They want winners, not losers. They'll look for another.

The only ones left are the people who want to see a tragedy – and the food and drink salesmen.

And what about the disciples? Heading for the hills, deserting him. Peter says, 'Ah nivver kent the man', then, quickly correcting himself, 'I never knew him'.

There is one last chance – a prisoner to be freed. 'Give us Barrabas!' And what will I do with Jesus of Nazareth?

'Crucify Him!'

Crowds are inspiring, exhilarating. Crowds are fickle, and dangerous.

Sometimes they strew his way,
and his sweet praises sing
Resounding all the day hosannas to their king.
Then 'Crucify!' is all their breath
And for his death they thirst and cry.

Jesus is alone.

They rise and needs will have
my dear lord done away;
A murderer they save, the Prince of Life they slay.
Yet cheerful he to suffering goes
that he his foes from thence might flee.

(Hymn 224)

It is through this journey, this lonely journey, that we track our salvation: because it is a journey of suffering love, beyond which lie astounding rumours of an empty tomb.

It is a lonely journey of transforming power.

And what about the entry of Hitler into Vienna?

Fifteen years later, the Nazi Messiah, hailed by 80 million people for his plans to set up a Reich that would last for a thousand years, was buried underneath the rubble of his own kingdom.

Yes, 100,000 lemmings can be wrong.

*　*　*

Today, in this Cathedral, seven people will confirm the vows made at their baptism. They will become part of the fellowship of the Man for Others. To join the Church these days is not to follow the crowd. Churchgoing isn't any more the flavour of the month. It's swimming against the tide.

But the crowd are not always right.
Our call is not to follow the crowd.
Our call is to follow Jesus.

CHAPTER 13

Big Boys
don't cry

Jesus wept.   John 11: 35

Weeping may endure for a night, but joy comes with the morning.
                                                                    Psalm 30: 5

ONE of the most poignant and powerful images of recent weeks was
the sight of one of our senior politicians in tears. Scottish Secretary
Ian Lang wept at the Tory Party conference in Inverness when he
heard of the death of his friend, John Smith, leader of the Labour
Party. Two things were remarkable:

1   A senior politician weeping over the death of a political opponent.
    It was as if a veil were suddenly lifted. There were things which
    transcended politics.
2   A man publicly in tears over the death of another man.

Why was this unusual? Because Big Boys Don't Cry.

Macho men don't, do they? (Sometimes they just have heart
attacks and live less long.) They would rather die (literally) than cry.

The model used to be John Wayne, on the frontier, killing and
destroying. George S Patton, the American war hero, said this: 'All real
American men love to fight.' It's dinned into us as boys.

Big boys don't cry … this is serious stuff. But why is it so rarely
talked about in church? Because the Church itself is riddled with it,
that's why. It comes into its theology and its hymns: 'Little Lord Jesus
no crying he made.' Really? Where did all this baloney come from?

All of this is exploded by two words in the Bible, the shortest text in the whole of the scriptures ... *Jesus wept.*

Does this mean that Jesus wasn't, er ... a real man? Was he – whisper it – a mammy's boy? After all, he didn't carry a weapon, he didn't fight, he wasn't in the image of John Wayne (who turned out not to be so gung-ho after all).

There is no problem about the masculinity of Jesus. The difference is that he didn't confuse strength with running around fighting people.

And he didn't confuse tears with weakness.

Jesus was a strong man who confronted the Romans and the Pharisees and the chief priests and all the others without violence. He was tough enough to face his own death. But he was also capable of tenderness, and love, and tears. That's why he wept at the tomb of his friend, Lazarus.

Then the Jews said: *See how he loved him.*

* * *

Switch to a later tomb.

The women had been weeping – but, then, women always do, don't they?

The men hadn't been weeping, but they had been full of self-pity. They shared a common loss, these women and men – they had lost the man they loved, and had followed. It was more than an ordinary bereavement. They had invested their lives in him – and their hopes had turned to ashes. Their hearts were wintry, grieving and in pain, even in this springtime.

Then some of the women, still grief-stricken, did something practical. They went to the tomb to anoint the body of Jesus.

(Isn't it interesting that in the Gospel story, it was the women who stood by the Cross after the men had gone? And it was the women who went to the tomb to do the needful.)

When they got there, they discovered that the tomb was empty. The body was gone. Where was he? John tells how Mary is looking,

looking. Then along comes a man. She looks at him through tear-filled eyes. He looks a bit like Jesus, but it can't be – after all, dead men don't walk. That's common sense.

She believes him to be the gardener ... until he speaks. And speaks again. And then she knows.

When the women rush back to tell the others, the men don't believe them. The men never do, do they? It's just hysterical women's talk, isn't it? It goes against all common sense!

(Isn't it also revealing that although it was women who stood by Jesus in his darkest hour, and were the first witnesses of his Resurrection, down through many centuries men have denied women the right to share fully in Christ's ministry.)

The men have to find out for themselves. So they go to the tomb. He is not there. He is risen!

Whatever happened that first Easter morning – and we only have a series of blurred pictures – that little community of men and women was transformed from a community of death into a community of life.

Their tears of sadness were transmuted into tears of joy.

Weeping may endure for a night, but joy comes with the morning.

But is all this simply a historic curiosity?

There are probably people in this Cathedral who spent last night weeping, or pacing the floor with worry. And I know that there are folk in this kirk who have endured severe losses in this past year – the death of a loved one, redundancy, hard problems with children.

The promise of the Gospel – and it goes right back to the Psalms – is that weeping endures for a night, but joy comes with the morning.

The night is a symbol – it may mean many nights, or even years: but the promise is that tears are not forever. Indeed, God promises: *I will wipe away all tears from their eyes ...*

What the story of Holy Week and Easter tells us – what the Gospel tells us – is that the weeping is for real, the pain is for real, the loss is for real, the bereavement is for real – and these things can't be wished away. Positive thinking won't do it. Wishful thinking won't do it.

The Cross of Jesus was a cross of pain and sorrow and tears. It was no make-believe.The Resurrection did not do away with the pain of Calvary: it transcended it, transformed it. And that is the promise of God.

The Gospel is only good news for us if it deals with the world as we experience it, not as we would like it to be.

What about the people of Northern Ireland in their long night of weeping? The promise to them is that joy will come in the morning. Some of them may never see that morning in their own life-time: they may only see it beyond death. But they will see it.

And what about South Africa? Many people have had long nights of weeping over the last half century or so, as justice for all people seemed like a dream. The promise is for them.

And what about people in Jerusalem, in the West Bank, in the Gaza Strip. The promise is for them. The night of weeping does not last for ever.

Resurrection is not a once and for all event. It is a repeated reality. Let me give you an example.

In Moscow in the time of Stalin, when millions were being sent to the Gulags for punishment and death, a huge political rally was held in one of the big stadiums. It lasted for three hours. People were compelled to go to it. Speaker after speaker denounced religion as the opiate of the people.

When the orators had finished, an old man in the crowd got up and shouted out an Easter refrain from the Russian Orthodox Church Easter liturgy. It fact we used it this morning: *Christ is Risen!* And the people shouted back: *He is risen indeed!*

In the midst of the night of weeping, there was a cry of hope ... *Christ is Risen!*

People in that crowd could not have predicted that fifty years later, the Berlin wall would crumble and the Communist government would be overthrown .... After the long night of weeping, the morning of joy.

But one experience of resurrection is not a quick fix. The peoples of Russia have found that unrestrained capitalism is not an answer any more than communism is, so they have to struggle to find new ways forward. But things can never be quite the same.

And how about our lives?

What about the husband and wife, whose marriage is wrecked beyond repair, and who feel themselves to be failures?

What about the person grieving a dead partner with whom they have shared their lives?

What about the parents, looking despairingly at the body of a dead child?

The faith at the heart of the Gospel is that God's tears are intermingled with our own. The tears of Jesus at the grave of his friend tell us this.

In Greek philosophy, one of the most important attributes of God was *apatheia*, impassibility. God could not suffer. There is an indifference about that god.

But a God who weeps is something else.

In Ian Lang's tears for John Smith, we glimpse something about the nature of humanity beyond politics.

In the tears of Jesus for Lazarus, we glimpse something of the nature of the heartbeat of our universe.

The word of Resurrection is a word of hope: a cry which says that ultimately, despite the present circumstances, God's love can never be defeated – that even the bonds of death have been broken, and that for us, yes even for us, there will be a glad morning, even though we can't see it breaking yet.

That chink of light can sustain us in the dark times. It won't solve all our problems. It won't make all the pain go away.

But once we take it into our being, nothing can ever be the same.

So it was with the disciples and friends of Jesus. Their night of weeping was transformed into a morning of joy: but that didn't mean they had an easy life. For some of them it meant torture and imprisonment, and even crucifixion.

But having tasted the Resurrection life, nothing could ever be the same. It was a promise of how things would be beyond death, beyond space and time, in the kingdom of God.

Easter is the most beautiful time of the Christian Year. Christmas is marvellous, and I love it, because it tells us of the birth of a child of promise. But if the child only grew up to die an unjust death, it would be a beautiful but ultimately tragic story. It would leave us with the disciples on Easter Saturday, despairing and without hope.

But we're not left there. Easter goes beyond the Cross and the pain. Joy comes in the morning. And the promise is for us.

When our hearts are wintry, grieving or in pain;
Thy touch can call us back to life again;
Fields of our hearts that dead and bare have been:
Love is come again,
like wheat that springeth green.

Hymn 278 (CH3)

Christ is risen:
He is risen indeed.

PART II

Short Story

A Day in the Death
of a Minister

A POST-MODERN POSTSCRIPT

IT was 20th May 2009, three years after the Church of England was privatised – (the Church of Scotland had been dealt with the year before) – and an eerie mist covered the land.

Sandy knew the details of the church controversies well. In fact, he was writing his own definitive history of them. He had studied the stories often enough in the library, going over the material time and again. It was how he passed his days, scribbling notes in his immaculate, italic writing. These things needed to be chronicled, even though few people were interested in such matters now. Here is what he had written down for posterity in his spiral-bound notebook:

The facts. The government had decided that the time had come to take on the Church of England, 'the last bastion of protected state privilege'. (Actually, that's not quite true. The greatest remaining state monopoly was the monarchy. When the rumours of a royal abdication were at their height, a secret paper had been presented to the cabinet, suggesting that the royal state monopoly should be broken up, and the monarchy itself put out to tender. Sealed bids would be invited. What a storm there was when the paper was leaked! It argued that it was illogical to exempt the monarchy and church from the changes which had 'brought fresh air sweeping through every other national institution'. It was time, it said, to let the same hurricane blow through even the so-called sacrosanct institutions. Oh to have been a fly on the wall in the cabinet room when the Queen did eventually abdicate! Apparently some ministers came to blows on the question of whether foreigners, blacks and homosexuals should be excluded from the bidding. No mention of disabled people: should they have been angry?)

So the denomination which used to be known as the 'Church of England' lost its protected status and privileges, and became The Episcopal Church (England). When Charles and Camilla succeeded to the throne, the rights and privileges of being the national church of England for ten years were put out to tender. The package not only included handling the Coronation service itself, but also the transport and catering franchises, as well as the television rights. The Mormon Church (England) with huge funds from America, and with powerful backing from omnipresent BSkyB Television and the Murdoch press, won the glittering prize. (The poor old Roman Catholic Church came second! It hadn't seemed so long ago since the Catholic Church had announced triumphally that it was in position to take over the role of England's national church. The Church of England had been at its weakest point, and some prominent royal defections had created the impression that all roads were leading to Rome. Then the 'caretaker' Pope John XXIV caused mayhem with his revelation from heaven in the middle of the night – women could be ordained as priests! What fun! The Anglican clergy who had joined Rome because their own church had decided to ordain women in 1993 were beside themselves. Couldn't have happened to nicer people. They were faced with a choice of joining the Free Kirk or the breakaway True Catholic Church, which took a lot of priests – and money – with it.)

A year earlier, the Church of Scotland had become The Presbyterian Church (Scotland). Its national status had been easier to disentangle, because there were fewer constitutional implications. There had been few protests of any significance. (The liberals in the church had been routed in the post-millennial evangelical revival. The Kirk's conservatives had seized the initiative, especially those who had adopted the fashionable American 'Evangelical Power' strategy. Evangelical Power breakfasts at Crieff! Evangelical Power Dressing! Evangelical Power Spectacles! They favoured a complete withdrawal from public issues and a concentration on private and personal spiritual power. They were indifferent to, and sometimes even hostile to, the Scottish parliament.)

Management consultants were brought in to look at the 'Kirk' (as it was still sentimentally known), and far-reaching changes were made. Looking at the strengths and weaknesses of the 150,000 strong body, the consultants identified three main market sectors – baptisms, weddings and funerals – in which The Presbyterian Church (Scotland) could go for growth. Accordingly, the church had been broken up into three separate self-contained divisions, under the overall direction of a Chief Executive. In order to regain its share of the market and compete effectively for the main franchises, the former Church of Scotland's old headquarters at 121 George Street, Edinburgh had been sold to Marks & Spencers, and custom-built premises erected at an industrial estate in Livingston. The sale of the Assembly Hall on the Mound raised a substantial sum, which was used to fund the appointment of Regional Growth Directors.

As part of the drive to make the Presbyterian church 'leaner and fitter', all remaining 'non viable' units were closed, and at least one 'Major Worship Centre' was designated for each Region. Ministers (called 'clergypersons', a hangover from an EC directive made before Britain left the Community in 2006 following John Redwood's stunning victory over Gordon Brown) were appointed to churches on three-year contracts, renewable annually at the discretion of the Regional Growth Directors. Each of the church's 150 pastors negotiated their own salary and conditions, but their pay was performance related. As part of the package, every clergyperson was given an annual recruitment target and undertook to do two weeks management training every year.

The consultants also decided, after extensive market research, that the church's image was too gloomy and negative. A new logo was designed with the slogan 'Smile with Jesus!', accompanied by a Mr Happy figure. Following a slick television advertising campaign (designed by advisers from the rapidly growing American Southern Baptist Church and funded by the Murdoch press), there was an immediate financial turnaround in the first year. (Why not sponsorship now? Why not the Hovis Communion?) The slimmed-down, more up-beat kirk had the confidence to look at smaller denominations with a view to takeover and expansion as part of its new Growth Strategy. It was rumoured that a bid was being prepared at the Livingston HQ for the assets of the ailing rumps of the Congregational Union (Scotland) and the Methodist Church (Scotland).

Can one imagine Mr Happy being crucified?
On second thoughts, yes.

As he reviewed his notes, Sandy sighed and wrote with a wry smile, *It is finished.*

He did not feel too much like Smiling with Jesus. There was no longer a regular bus service to his town, and no trains had run there for years. A car was necessary, but he could not afford one, not with petrol at £20 a gallon and £1000 a year road tax. It was all right for people in work with their high salaries and only 12 pence in the pound income tax – a guaranteed election winner for Mr Redwood – but the means-tested pension left nothing over once the huge heating bills had been paid. All these years on the minimum stipend had left him poorly off.

He had become a minister in 1959. He had a vocation then. He sighed now when he recalled his zeal as a young man, leading crusades on behalf of his people against dampness in the high-rise flats, and against the money-lenders who preyed upon the poorest in the community. He was bold then, angry about injustice. Supported by his wife, Agnes, who had Parkinson's disease ('*Agnes Dei*' he used to call her, affectionately; their chief regret was that they had no children), he had led his congregation into the community. The long hours and continual availability had exhausted him, as had the intractability of the never-ending problems facing him. After twenty years in that first parish, he come close to breakdown. The rest of his ministry was spent in a linked country parish, working hard, caring for the people, trying to build bridges between the church and the community, trying in vain to halt the decline in church membership.

What had troubled him more deeply, though, was a much wider, more ominous corrosive gnawing. He had felt acutely the silent but inexorable disintegration of any sense of shared values. As a sensitive and caring man, he could feel within his being the turning of people away from each other, a retreat into private, individual concerns. The large numbers of unemployed, the homelessness and the growing drug dependency had given the country a very shadowy and ominous feel. Many people were wealthy, but most seemed to be under continual stress at work. Their homes were not just their castles, but fortresses. It was as if people had become blinded, as if they were in a deep mist, under a spell, and did not even realise the extent of their loss.

When he retired, he felt something of a failure. His ideals had not been realised. It was the death of Agnes, three years into the brash new millennium, that led Sandy into his deepest despair. He felt humiliated by the fact that he had not been able to afford proper medical care. The embarrassing questions at the hospital about his finances, the endless form-filling, the poverty of his health insurance arrangements, and the knowledge that health care for the likes of him was dependent on a national fundraising lottery made Agnes's terminal illness all the harder to bear. His anger – the old anger that had once come out in his dealings with landlords and loan sharks – had suddenly erupted in the hospital.

'This is a f...... disgrace!' he had shouted, uncharacteristically, at the consultant. (He only swore on exceptional occasions.)

'I'm surprised at you, a minister,' the consultant said, sadly.

After this, he had become a recluse, studying the details of obscure ecclesiastical debates in the local library, writing endlessly in his spiral-bound notebook. The *Scotsman* and *Herald* had become regional Murdoch journals. Someone had to tell the truth.

*   *   *

He walked on through the town, past the old kirk. It had closed some two years previously. Non-viable. Most people could not afford to travel into the Major Worship Centre, though there was talk of a mini-bus coming out to pick up those without cars. Sandy used to go to the old kirk after he retired until the day, not long after Agnes's death, when the smart young minister, who came every second Sunday from a nearby town, played the Twenty-third Psalm on the guitar and insisted that the mainly geriatric congregation clap hands to the rhythm. He had introduced the 'California Blessing' – which had succeeded and outdone the 'Toronto Blessing' – and had invited the congregation to laugh hysterically with him under the influence of the Spirit, and even to bark (only if they wished). The old kirk was now a gleaming 'Opportunity Centre' run by the burgeoning 'Opportunity Knocks Enterprise'.

His feet took him to the former Co-operative Society building. It was now the 'Free Choice Centre', run by Human Choice plc. It gave advice on abortion and euthanasia (fees payable only at point of execution). He found himself going in.

'Which service are you interested in, Mr Latimer?' asked the smart young man.

'Well, it's not likely to be abortion, is it?' said Sandy, without a flicker of expression.

The smart young man smiled wanly, but tolerantly. He had been on a training course on the subject of dealing with difficult clients.

'Euthanasia.'

The smart young man gave him a glossy leaflet entitled *The Choice is Yours*.

'Would you like the laser film that goes with it?' he asked, brightly.

'No. I don't even know what a laser film is.'

'If you want to follow the matter through after you've read the literature, we'll provide a counsellor to take you through the options.'

'Wonderful … counsellor,' said Sandy, again without a flicker of expression.

'What?' said the young man.

*   *   *

The old minister left the Free Choice Centre and shuffled towards the library. He wanted to read more about the history of the Free Kirk struggle. The Wee Free Choice Kirk! How about that for a name! He laughed aloud, till he was suddenly reminded that it was Assembly time for The Presbyterian Church (Scotland). The Assembly – which hardly rated a paragraph in the *Herald* and *Scotsman* – was a three-day event, over a long weekend in Livingston. It was advertised as a 'caring and sharing festival', with Moody and Sankey hymns and modern choruses interspersing the inspirational talks by the Regional Growth Directors and the motivational seminars on time manage-ment. Mr Happy beamed above it all.

Although he had made fun of it at the time, Sandy thought with nostalgia of the solemn church-and-state ceremony of the General Assembly of the Church of Scotland on the Mound, and the intensity and passion of some of the debates. It all seemed so interesting now (even though he had often been bored at the time). He thought of the times when he and Agnes had attended the Assembly Garden Party at Holyrood Palace. The event seemed to be always sunny in his memory! He remembered the day when one senior minister of the Kirk, who, in a panic as he realised that his false teeth were stuck to a meringue as the Queen approached, threw meringue and teeth behind a bush and faced Her Majesty with flashing gums.

As he crossed the road, Sandy found himself laughing maniacally, so loudly that people turned round in the street.

The car came towards him at speed, swerving, skidding. Sandy swayed backwards into its path, and he ended up on the bonnet, carried along for about two hundred yards before he came crashing off on to the roadway.

The young driver, distressed, jumped out. Music roared out of the open door. 'Clap! Clap! Clap your hands! Jesus our king is coming back!' A familiar Happy logo was on the back window of the car.

Crowds gathered round as Sandy lay on the road,

'It wisnae your fault, son,' someone said to the driver, putting a sympathetic hand on to his camel-hair car coat. 'That crazy auld bugger must have a death wish.'

The driver moved his head down to the old man. Lying there, Sandy looked as vulnerable as a child.

'I'm a clergyperson,' the young man said. 'Is there anything I can do?'

It was only then that Sandy recognised him as the young minister who had played the guitar in his church.

It all came back. The Lord's my Shepherd. Clap, Clap ….

The old man's lips moved. The voice was faint. The driver moved closer.

'Is there anything I can do?' the young man repeated plaintively, anxiously.

'You can turn off that f…… music,' whispered the old man. (This was an exceptional occasion.)

'Would you like me to say a prayer?' said the young man, not hearing.

'Only if you promise not to bark.'

The young minister took out his Bible, and read the words of Jesus: *You have not chosen me, I have chosen you.*

'The Wee Free Choice Kirk!' uttered the old man, grimacing.

'What?' said the young minister.

Clap! Clap! Clap your hands …

'It is finished,' groaned the old man, as the sirens mercifully drowned out the sound of the chorus. '*Agnes Dei,*' he muttered, with a faint smile.

'What?' said the young minister.

'Poor demented bugger,' said the man in the crowd.

*   *   *

All this happened on 20th May 2009, three years after the Church of England was privatised.

And an eerie mist enshrouded the land.

PART III

Newspaper Articles

Credit
where Debt
is due

IT'S not really all that long ago – though psychologically it feels aeons ago – since the days when the local bank manager saw it as his job to keep his clients out of debt. Dressed in sober suit, often silver-haired, he – and it was always a he – would summon the male-factor to a meeting at the bank.

The encounter was usually not simply a friendly chat between con-senting adults. It was a meeting between unequals. The atmosphere was often more akin to the heidie's room. The Lochgelly strap was not in evidence, but it might as well have been. The whole banking scene was part of Presbyterianism's Scottish heyday: moral and fiscal rectitude, laced with a hint of divine judgment. Getting into debt was not just unfortunate; it was a sin.

Some privileged people were allowed to borrow a bit of the filthy stuff, but only after a seventh-degree grilling and a character check that would have eliminated most of the saints.

Then the tornadoes of change which blew through society swept through the financial institutions as well. Credit was the name of the new game in town. The City of London became one of the great financial powerhouses of the world. Fortunes could be made quickly, simply by knowing when to buy and sell money.

Styles changed with the fast-moving developments, even in the conservative banking world. Hang loose, baby! Unbutton that waist-coat! Bank managers became less avuncular, more informal. Call me 'Freddy'! You want to borrow money? Sure! This is the bank that likes to say Yes!

Suddenly, the world was full of retired bank managers – too old at 48 for this dynamic, competitive business. Clients were bombarded with glossy mail, offering them huge loans with apparently few security checks. I was offered a loan through the post the other day, so that I could buy a yacht I'd apparently always dreamed about.

One of the outcomes of this revolution is that the job of your friendly neighbourhood youthful all-singing, all-dancing bank manager is now to sell you money. Bank staff are under phenomenal pressure.

A lot of it has been good. Life on tick has enabled businesses to expand, and young couples to have decent housing. It has supported creative risk-taking. It has provided the social and economic matrix for an exponential rise in living standards.

Prudential Presbyterianism, which has been a long time a-dying, is floating lifelessly in the water, along with socialism. Both have probably deserved their fates, having feasted off dead carcasses for too long. The all-conquering ideology of the market has won the war.

There have been many casualties. Personal debt is one of the major social problems this country faces. The lure of easy money is hard to resist. The insistent pressures of advertising build up till they breach the stoutest dam, especially in the season of goodwill. 'Santa's Little Helper' was the recent advertising slogan of one major credit card company.

The corrosive effect of chronic debt destroys relationships and even communities. Santa's Little Helper can pave the way for a descent into hell, to reintroduce a frightening wee Presbyterian word.

When payback time comes, the going can get really rough. I've seen it in the Glasgow housing schemes. The man with the scar lurking at the corner is wielding a baseball bat. He does not bring good tidings of peace and goodwill.

THE middle classes don't face bats, but nice Freddy at the Bank Which Likes to Say Yes can turn into Freddy Krueger as *Nightmare on Elm Street* begins. There is no such thing as a free Biro. But at least the law prevents us getting into more debt than we can handle. If this starts to happen, we are declared bankrupt.

There is no safety net for a country. The debts just continue to soar, as some of the poorest countries in the world have found to their cost. In the 1970s, the oil-producing countries formed a cartel and forced up the oil prices. They became very rich, and put their money into Western banks.

The banks used the money to make more. They contacted Third World countries and offered them easy loans. They did little checking. Countries, some with corrupt leadership, desperate to develop higher living standards, took big loans. Then interest rates in the West jumped sky high, at the same time as the price of Third World exports plummeted. Corporate negative equity spelt ruin.

Now Unicef estimates that 500,000 children a week die because of the debt crisis. Today's children are paying for the folly of a world that went mad twenty years before they were born. In Uganda the government spend £1.60 per person on health care, and £19 per person on debt repayments. Each person in the Third World owes about £250 to the West – more than a year's wages for most people. The poor are caught in a debt trap that they cannot possibly get out of.

The Jubilee 2000 movement, while fully acknowledging the responsibility of those who took out the loans, argues that the Third Millennium presents a unique opportunity to come to terms with the issue of complicity, and make a historic, one-off gesture which will transform the possibilities for the world's poor.

This coalition of Churches and aid agencies which have a tremendous track record in the developing world, feel that this could be a more fitting celebration of 2000 years of Christianity than the building of a £780 million dome in London.

Christian Aid television commercials on the subject have been banned. Too political, apparently. You can show British children in adverts lusting after the most expensive gear, but you cannot show children dying in poverty as a result of massive debt. Mustn't upset Santa's Little Helpers, must we? We are being subliminally politicised. Thus the victory of global market forces is complete until the next Stock Exchange crash.

We are being brainwashed in the name of an ideology which is no less insidious because it presents itself innocently as an apolitical view of the way the 'real world' is. Isn't it time we woke up?

26 December 1997

This Way
lies
Madness

TWO pictures haunt the mind this week. First, the look of relief on the face of English au pair Louise Woodward in a Boston courtroom as judge Hiller Zobel announces her freedom. Second, the tortured grimace of Scottish paedophile Steven Leisk as he is led out of Aberdeen High court to begin a 25 year jail sentence.

Then two contrasting scenes. In the Rigger pub in Elton, Louise Woodward's home village, people cheer and cry and laugh and hug one another. The banners 'Louise is Innocent' fly. Outside the High Court in Aberdeen, a baying mob cries 'scum' and 'animal' as Leisk is led away.

Woodward is known to the world simply as 'Louise'. Leisk is referred to as a 'monster'. Yet what links these two people is this: after due process of law, they have both been declared responsible, in some form or another, for the death of a child.

The two cases are totally different, of course, but they raise issues about instant judgement by emotion, the power of television, and how we value our children.

The post-Diana mood in Britain is a strange one. It is as if there is a restless, gathered sense of emotion searching for a collective focus, any focus. Louise Woodward as icon? The notion is grotesque. The *Sun* newspaper, in full, nauseating, populist mode, called her – seriously – 'the light of our lives'. This way lies madness.

As the Massachusetts court opera soap opera developed, Louise Woodward became the frightened victim, set up by evil forces. She became the fragrant English girl scapegoated by twisted, brash American justice. As the public emotional head of steam developed, television came into its own, feeding the frenzy. Cameras were in the Rigger pub, of course. Wonder why the vicar was always in the front of the crowd? Because the television director placed him there, that's why.

People who saw and heard only a fragment of the evidence moved to instant judgement.

They just *knew*; they didn't need to trouble with such a distracting thing as evidence. Not only was Louise completely innocent, it was the parents who were guilty. Either the father did it, or the mother. The instant judges just knew by the look of the parents, who didn't show enough emotion, weep enough.

Television is a deceptive and sometimes destructive medium. It selects and distorts, while presenting the image of objectivity. Yes, the camera can lie.

When Louise was found guilty, after the failure of her theatrical defence team's high-risk strategy, the conspiracy theories took wings. The Internet became the place where grievers – and grievance-merchants – met. Money poured in to the 'Free Louise' fund. Newspapers ran phone-ins. The au pair looked lonely and frightened. Goodbye England's Rose? The bizarre mythology doesn't bear thinking about.

Justice does not come by way of phone-ins, slogans or opinion polls, but by compassionate and careful weighing up of evidence. The much maligned American justice system delivered a verdict which was humane and – so far as one can ever understand these things – fair. The confused and sad

Louise Woodward will eventually come home, but not, please God, as a heroine.

In the meantime, the real victim of the tragedy, Matthew Eappen, is in his tiny grave. He will not grow old, as we that are left ....

IN Aberdeen, there is no sympathy for Steven Leisk as he starts a life sentence. His deeds have been truly vile, and he must be kept away from children for life. Yet a searchlight on his life reveals a pathetic character. Brutally abused himself as a child, he was traumatised by his work as a medical orderly in the army in the Falklands, clearing up dismembered bodies. He will now be repeatedly attacked by prisoners until, perhaps, he breaks and commits suicide. There will be few tears shed for him, on television or elsewhere.

The understandable demonising and hounding of paedophiles masks the fact that most child abuse happens in the home, committed by trusted relatives: or, as we see time after time, in public institutions registered for the care for children. The public humiliation of known offenders conceals the simple fact that if every 'monster' and every slightly dodgy au pair in the world were strung up, the mass of child abuse would still be left undealt with.

There are further disturbing questions about other ways in which children are abused emotionally. Why are kids regularly handed over to untrained people all day and every day? Why is the care of young children one of the most undervalued professions? Why is it so often essential in a two-parent family that both parents work full-time? If it is essential for economic survival reasons, why are so many jobs paid so poorly? If it is not for economic survival, what values and expectations underlie these decisions? What support is there for single parents struggling to bring up kids? What has happened to the dream of a society where both parents can work part-time and share in the upbringing of the children? What has happened to the notion of work sharing? Why is it that Britain has the longest working-hours in Europe, meaning that parents are exhausted by the time they get home, with little left over for the children?

All these issues affect children very deeply. So too does the emotional holocaust of family break-up and divorce. There are times when divorce is the only compassionate last resort, but the emotional, psychological and economic costs of a high divorce rate are overwhelmingly damaging for children's lives. A culture in which abortion plays such a prominent part is hardly a child-friendly culture either.

These are complex, difficult and uncomfortable questions, and it is easier to mount a campaign to rescue an au pair or hound a 'monster' than it is to address them with honesty and determination. Despite all the public sentimentality, we are not producing a society which nurtures and cares for children. Is there any emotion to spare?

14 November 1997

Peedie
Bairn
of Bethlehem

YOUR Christmas quiz-starter for ten. First question – *according to the Bible, how many wise men were there?*
(a) two
(b) three
(c) eleven, with three substitutes

Question two – *were the Wise Men*
(a) spin doctors
(b) kings
(c) transvestites

Question three – *was there in the stable*
(a) an ox
(b) a donkey
(c) beef on the bone

Question four – *outside the stable was there*
(a) a Christmas tree
(b) a robin
(c) a DSS inspector

The answer to all these questions is: *we haven't a clue*. The biblical story doesn't tell us any of these things. Most of the stuff about Christmas is Victorian hokum.

The best antidote is a viewing of the hilarious Monty Python 'Life of Brian'. The film opens with Three Wise Men on camels, arriving at a tumbledown house. They go in, put down their expensive gifts and prostrate themselves before a new-born child, much to the bafflement of the bairn's watching single mother. Minutes later, they come back angrily and snatch the gifts away again. Wrong hoose.

* * *

Here's another Christmas question – *who was present at the birth of Jesus?*
(a) Joseph
(b) The little drummer boy
(c) The Child Support Agency

According to the artists of San Gregoria, Naples, there was another hovering holy presence – Diana, Princess of Wales. That's right. In the ceramic crib scenes which are selling faster than mince pies, Diana is in there beside Joseph and the BSE-free oxen, ready for Bethlehem's first photo-call.

I am not making up a single word of this. I have not dined on magic mushrooms. Diana in the crib scene! Pass me the Blue Nun. The world is steadily going off its corporate heid. Will the *Sun* set up a reader's phone-in? Vote Now! Who do *you* think should be in the Holy Family, holding the baby? The Spice Girls? Paula Yates? Louise Woodward? (*Oops! Maybe not.*)

Personally, I vote for the Scotland football team's Craig Brown (checking with Joseph if there's any Scottish blood in the family, just in case ....)

* * *

I love Christmas, including the hokum, but I do want to say something which is on my heart. It arises out of a conversation I had at a Christmas lunch a couple of days ago. Much wine had been taken, and truth was being spoken. The woman opposite me, in her sixties, told me about her daughter, who was divorced, with a young child. The wee one asked her grandmother, 'Are you and grandpa married for ever?'

Grandma replied in the affirmative.

'I hope so,' said the grandchild wistfully. 'If not, my mummy will be very upset.'

This article is not a plea to go back to some imaginary golden age

when mum and dad and the kids were like these cereal adverts. It never was as simple as that. There are times when divorce is the only humane resort left. I have friends in partnerships which are very irregular as far as the traditional norms are concerned, and a lot of these relationships have more integrity than many marriages.

But I wince as the Christmas newsletters come in, with more and more news of family break-ups. I am not talking about blame here, but about pain – especially for broken-hearted children. I think about the 'peedie ones', as people in Orkney call children with great affection.

Despite our sentimentality at Christmas time, we are not a child-nurturing society. We have lost the plot. Childhood is the foundation-time, the time when security and confidence are formed, and we do not provide enough support for those, men or women, whose demanding vocation it is to bring up children. The flaw in the government's recent thinking was the assumption that every lone parent should go out to work. The demeaning of what is involved in bringing up kids is the worst thing our society does.

I suspect that Diana is in that daft Neapolitan crib because she is the personal representation of a modern communal yearning – herself the product of a broken home, divorced, a mother of hurt boys, restlessly trying to find happiness. She is more accessible in today's world than a Blessed Virgin. She is the Princess of Postmodernity.

There is a shadow over Christmas. There are too many homes with pained and hurting young ones at this season. As a society, we need to think again. Co-creating and nurturing children is an awesome responsibility. The price of the pursuit of individual happiness must not be borne by silently damaged children, whose greatest need is not expensive presents, but love.

CHRISTMAS Eve. The floodlit St Magnus Cathedral in Orkney, like many churches in the land, will be crowded with people – sober, drunk, believing, disbelieving, celebrating, hurting, like a cast from a George Mackay Brown short story.

We will sing familiar carols. Then at midnight a candle will be lit. Time will stand still. The corporate yearning will be almost tangible. In the silence, our prayer is that the peedie bairn of Bethlehem will touch our wounded hearts.

19 December 1997

Cult of
the new
goddess Diana

THE cult of Diana once represented an important part of religious orthodoxy. Its headquarters was the lovely temple in the city of Ephesus, and its worship and artefacts produced a lucrative living for the local silversmiths. The story is all there in the New Testament. The apostle Paul and his followers were starting to cause panic with their stories about a charismatic Jewish teacher, Jesus of Nazareth, who met a violent death after challenging the Establishment and breaking all known protocols by embracing the lepers and the outcasts. Sophisticated civic and religious leaders were appalled as the Nazarene cult began to spread amid a kind mass hysteria – people even claimed to have seen the crucified teacher.

What was even worse was that trade was being affected. The Ephesian tourist board called a crisis meeting to deal with the danger posed by the crass new religion. The leading hyper-ventilating silversmith said: 'Not only is this trade of ours in danger of falling into disrepute, but also the temple

of the great goddess Diana – whom all Asia and the world worship – may be despised and her magnificence destroyed.' The whipped-up crowds then rushed out into the streets shouting 'Great is Diana of the Ephesians!' and grabbed the friends of Paul.

And that was before the tabloids.

At the time, it was thought the Jesus cult would peter out quickly. The authorities totally misread the situation. The rapid spread of the Jewish sect provoked a shaking of the foundations. From apparently insignificant origins, the outlawed Jesus movement went on to shape what we now know as Western civilisation. Its representatives would put crowns on the heads of emperors, build great cathedrals, and produce great music and art as well as great saints. Has the 2000 year old circle turned? Is the cult of the new goddess Diana about to overthrow the established orthodoxy? New cult, new culture?

No, say the official representatives. The new Diana cult is an ephemeral thing – an insignificant, shallow, vulgar movement, whipped up by the media. Some adjustments will have to be made, but this thing will pass.

What makes a cult is the adoration of a charismatic leader, usually dead at an early age. Death transforms the teacher, removing him or her from historical time and space to the mythic dimensions. The leader's faults usually disappear or are relativised. Think even of John Smith, a very unlikely figure for cult status. Before his untimely death, he was often presented in the media as a boring bank manager in a suit. After death, he was, hey!, convivial, brilliant, the best Prime Minister we never had! Now his grave on the holy island of Iona is sinking under the pressure of pilgrim feet. (As you read this column I hope that this genuinely great Scotsman's 'unfinished business' has been completed with a confident flourish.)

While she was alive, Princess Diana was often portrayed in the media as a scheming, needy manipulator of the tabloid black arts. If she had gone on to marry the playboy Dodi of controversial family history, and perhaps ended up twice-divorced, gin-soaked, and wizened, would there have been national mourning? (For that matter, if Jesus had died at the age of 75 of pneumonia, would there

have been an all-conquering, all-singing, all-dancing, all-burning-at-the-stake Church?)

CAN the new cult of the ever-young, eternally beautiful Diana overthrow creaking orthodoxy, in the same way as the radical Jewish movement overturned the traditional Diana cult two millenniums ago? I suspect not. (Though when will the resurrection appearances begin?)

To understand the new phenomenon, we need to turn not to the old hunting goddess, but to another Greek god, Narcissus, the silently conquering god of the modern age. According to Greek myth, Narcissus was a handsome young Thespian who caught sight of himself in a pool. He immediately fell in love with his own reflection, and refused to leave the spot. He died of languor, and turned into a flower. He did not love himself – he loved the image of himself, and it was the death of him.

As far as I can understand the situation, Princess Diana did not like her flesh-and-blood self very much, but fell in love with her own image. That is why the goddess of hunting needed the hunting pack with cameras. She really existed only when she was in the public eye. That is why she could not stay out of the limelight. In real life, according to her brother, she was searching desperately for affirmation, often through wonderfully effective charitable work; and also by means of astrology, reflexology, and other New Age nostrums.

So much of public life today is a hall of mirrors, image piled upon reflected image. People who had never met the historical, compassionate, needy, vengeful Diana fell in love with her image. As her faults fell away in martyrdom, her awful death became the blessed assumption of a queen of heaven. At the end of the day, though, she was queen only of the pervasive, world-wide realm of Psychobabylonia. That judgment may seem harsh; I believe it to be true, and not unkind.

Is that all that needs to be said? Is it back to business as usual? Absolutely not. While I personally don't believe that the Diana cult has the substance to produce the revolution we need, it taps into a wider, deeper, yearning and searching. The Church was found wanting long ago – its unintelligible, exclusive church-speak and its wounding, dinosauric Catholic-Protestant battles making it of marginal influence on many areas of modern life. The crown is askew on the monarch's head, and the Westminster pin-stripe bearpit can no longer do the business.

Even in the reflecting modern halls of Narcissus, the image of a beautiful and compassionate young woman reaching out to the lepers and the Aids victims haunts the mind with unbearable poignancy. But the hunted, hunting Diana cannot bear the weight of the aspirations and longing of all our dreams. The best way to honour a genuinely inspiring memory is not to worship at a shrine, but to protect her sons and make the world a kinder place.

But be sure; the foundations are being shaken once again. The old orthodoxies cannot bear the weight of the new situation either, without radical transformation.

It is time for the authorised silversmiths to start checking their insurance policies.

12 September 1997

High Office, Low Deeds

IN these days of public humilia-tions and dreaded 'outings', this Great Column is going to have to face its public in confessional mode. It is necessary to begin with an embarrassing declaration about youthful indiscretions. Are the cameras ready? The lights? Let the sweating commence.

Gulp. Here goes. Give me a glass of water. That's better. Now here is my deposition. When I was about 12 or 13, being raised by wolves and roaming free among the pit bings of Cowdenbeath, I and my pals used to go on shop-ping expeditions. The only snag was we didn't have any money to buy things with. (Aye, it was tough in these days, living in cardboard boxes, fighting the dogs for scraps, running around in bare feet, and ....)

Not having cash did not stop us shopping. We would saunter into Woolworths, one of the group would distract the shop lassie, and we would snitch a few items from the counter. Then we would saunter out, past the sign saying 'Thank you for shopping at Woolworths',

and distribute the spoils, us latter-day Fife Robin Hoods.

We got away with it, and we became bolder. We decided to plan a raid on Dunfermline Woolies. This was really was the big-time. The game-plan worked again, and we sloped off with some pocket French dictionaries. Just what every 12-year-old in Cowdenbeath wanted.

You may think that this was stealing. But it wasn't, not on my definition of the word 'stealing', the one that my expensive law-yers wrote out for me. I called it 'consuming', or 'redistributing wealth'. Okay?

Why am I telling you all this? First of all, because I have a col-umn to fill. Secondly, after the daily diet of revelations about Bill Clinton, your jaded appetites will need stimulated by something even more sensational. And, thirdly, because I am thinking of running for the office of Prime Minister.

I'm not a member of a politi-cal party, but that doesn't matter. I'm going to run as 'the People's Premier'. Seeing youse are the people, you will vote for me. Clever, eh? I'll fight on the platform of redistribution of wealth, though I'll come down really hard on stealing. I will flog petty pilferers, string 'em up, in fact.

But if I'm running for Prime Minister, why make this public confession? The reason is that once I announce my candidature, the moral bloodhounds will be out to check out my past, my present, and my future. No dark stone will be left unturned. So, I'm getting my retaliation in first.

But, I hear you cry plaintively, you haven't told us whether you were caught and punished after your 'shopping' expeditions, and whether your career in crime extended to taking part in the Great Train Robbery? You may then inquire: is all that stuff about pilfering really true? And are you really going to run for Premier?

Okay, let me make yet another confession. I made up that stuff about being Prime Minister. It strikes me that no one with any sense nowadays will run for high office. Bill Clinton is an extreme case, since he has wounded himself so spectacularly and so publicly, but how many people would care to have their lives trawled over under the glare of camera lights? In most people's dark inner cupboards there are a few skeletons

waiting to clatter out in the most embarrassing fashion – what the liturgy calls 'sins of omission and commission'.

When John Major was Prime Minister, a youthful liaison was disinterred and turned into screaming headlines. His own family's love lives were put under the spotlight.

When Tony Blair became leader of the Labour Party, tabloid journalists were out in force, going over his past. Former teenage girlfriends and classmates were tracked down in the hope of turning up sensational news of even a youthful back-row fumble. If he is still in office when his children are teenagers, you can be sure that every relationship of theirs will be under scrutiny, with cheque book at the ready to loosen tongues. This is a very high price to pay for political power.

Blair passed the scrutiny tests. With the connivance of his own spin doctors, he was then built up into a kind of Superman. That is when the new set of troubles start. The sight of a person continually walking on the political waters eventually becomes boring. The sport is to gun him down. If things go wrong, the anger knows no bounds. Superman becomes Supervillain.

None of this makes for good

government. Why should any person of ability put him or herself forward for public office when they know that their lives will be raked over, and that their families will be compelled to live out private agonies in the public spotlight?

It is a strange paradox that at a time when sexual mores are changing so much, the private lives of public figures should come in for such close scrutiny. The editors who sit in judgment are not all conspicuous examples of moral rectitude.

If we only want people who have lived faultless lives to represent us, then we will be ruled by John Gummers. If we turn ferociously on politicians because they fail to deliver the whole package of human happiness, we condemn ourselves to leadership of stunning mediocrity. If we encourage a political culture of blame which pretends that every problem is solvable, we tread a wheel of perpetual disappointment. If we support the slavering investigators of private lives, we get the politics we deserve.

Archbishop William Temple, was berated by a lady about the indiscretions of some Anglican priests. When she demanded to know why the quality of priests was so low, the Archbishop looked his questioner in the eye and replied: 'Because we only have the laity to choose from.'

By the way, I didn't get caught. If any of Fife's finest are reading this I will come quietly. As for the Great Train Robbery, my lips are sealed.

25 September 1998

Prayer
for the
Broken People

IT'S 2 am, the temperature is 36°C, and I'm shivering under the mosquito net. Sunstroke! (Hey, I'm not looking for sympathy from people in Scotland in February.) As I lie there, I'm reminded of the plaque in St Mary's Church, Madras – the oldest Anglican church east of Suez – which says of the late Lieutenant W H Atkinson: 'The change of climate required by a service of 32 years having been deferred until too late a season, he sank under the intense heat of the Red Sea and died within a few days after his retirement.'

So, that's it then: Calvinist revenge for frolicking in the sea at Covalam beach, while people shiver at home after gathering winter fuel. Such frivolity was bound to get its comeuppance in the great scheme of things. At least, I reflect in melancholic vein, I might be worth a plaque in that church alongside such heroes of the Empire as the (genuine) Guy Lushington Prendergast and the Rev. Walter Posthumous Powell. I feel a tad posthumous myself right now.

Two days later I find I'm not dead. I'm bright pink and breathing normally. I will live to fax another column.

I'm living at the Kerela United Theological College in Trivandrum at the southernmost tip of India. I talk with staff and students about the problems facing the Church of South India as a minority body. On Sunday I get on the back of a scooter, with a college lecturer in full white priestly robes at the controls. I have what my musician daughter would call a 'preaching gig'.

In Madras I had spoken to a packed, fairly affluent Indian congregation in St Andrews Kirk: this Sunday is the opposite end of the spectrum.

The congregation is in a Dalit community. The Dalits are the outcasts, literally the broken people, the Untouchables. They have struggled to keep this church alive.

I speak in English, and the sermon is translated into Malayalam. It sounds more profound in Malayalam. Then Holy Communion, in a foreign tongue, but we all understand the Galilean speech. I am touched by the sight of these poor people kneeling for communion. *The Body of Christ, broken for you.* It comes alive for me in a new and revealing way. It comes alive for me in a new and revealing way. The *Body of Christ.* I am reminded of the shit-encrusted bodies cared for by the nuns and volunteers in Mother Teresa's Home for the Dying: the body of the Christ who was crucified for touching the Untouchables and breaking bread with sinners – now in broken bread and poured wine for the broken people, the children of God. *Kyrie Eleison,* Christ have mercy.

I am taken out to an ashram founded by a Bethany Roman Catholic priest, Father Gabriel, and Tom Sutherland, an Australian Presbyterian layman. Tom is one of the most impressive men I have ever met: very gentle, with a totally unpretentious spiritual authority.

There are crowds of people wanting to speak to him. The ashram provides work for many women, all of them poor, many of them abandoned. There is a hostel for people who are ill or destitute or mentally handicapped, and a small pharmacy for the sick.

Tom explains quietly how, when someone is seriously ill, their family and friends have to rush around to buy medical equipment for the operation, which will not happen until every rupee has been raised. Poor people cannot raise the money, and the ashram does what it can. *Whatever ye did for the least of these, ye did unto me.* When I compare what is happening with so much of our increasingly hollow celebrity culture at home, I feel humbled.

Following another long train journey, it's back to Madras, staying with dear friends from Glasgow days, Raj and Jaishree Singh. Their daughter, Arthi, is now an elegant 11-year-old, and my godson Jayant, baptised in Govan Parish Church 10 years ago, is a spirited lad. Raj is young to be consultant in respiratory medicine at one of the Madras hospitals, and he is heading up a programme to improve the care of asthma sufferers. We talk into the night about the problems facing the world's biggest democracy as it moves towards polling day.

Now my preparations are homewards, to think again. What a rich experience this visit has been! I have been frozen in Darjeeling, and eaten alive by malaria-bearing mosquitoes. (If I become delirious, will you be able to tell the difference?) I've travelled thousands of miles and have had several near-death experiences in the traffic in Calcutta.

I've shared accommodation with cockroaches, ants, lizards, and fireflies, and have seen the odd snake. I've taught two precious kids in Madras to say 'Nae bother, pal' in convincing West of Scotland accents. I've been in Hindu and Buddhist temples, and have learned more about other faiths. I've seen unbearable poverty, and have witnessed examples of heroism and saintliness which have moved me deeply.

I've eaten spicy South Indian food off banana leaves with my right hand, and I've had the odd touch of the notorious Delhi belly. I've sweated in the plains and been awed by the grandeur of the Himalayas. I feel as if I have met or seen a big chunk of India's 960 million inhabitants.

It has been a tumultuous experience, this trip; part-holiday, part-work, part-writing assignment, part-pilgrimage. I have been challenged, stretched, and confirmed. I have been invaded by the grace of this magical, glorious, disturbing, distressing country, but not, I hope, by its dysentery. My senses have been ravaged.

So now I get mentally prepared to open up again the cornucopia of delights which is Scotland in February. As mystics both East and West would observe enigmatically: maybe aye, maybe no.

Or again, as Arthi and Jayant would say in deepest, darkest Madras: nae bother, pal.

13 February 1998

Life, Death and the Earth

THERE is not enough daylight in Orkney right now; not even enough to bury the dead. We've had a lot of deaths this past while and, because of the short daylight 'window' in these dark December days, there has had to be a queuing system for burials.

Death in a small island community is inescapable. There are no euphemisms. People whose ancestors have lived off the land for centuries have learned to live with the rhythm of the seasons, with light and darkness, with life and death. There is no crematorium here, and no demand for one: something to do with these same rhythms, and the relationship between life, death, and the earth which produces Orkney's rich harvest in days when the island light is breathtakingly luminous.

Walk down Kirkwall's main street, and the death notices are up in the windows of the florists' shops. People stand around them, talking in low voices about the deceased – about their close family, their cousins, their great grandparents, all the way back to the original Orcadian Adam Firth and Eve Flett. To speak ill of anyone here is to risk the wrath of at least 200 people, and that's just the immediate family.

Funerals are communal occasions, and the winter heightens the sense of sad but sacred Northern theatre. To follow the hearse from the Viking St Magnus cathedral out of the old St Olaf cemetery, where the rain comes horizontally from storm-troubled Scapa, is to participate in an elemental community ritual. To stand at freshly dug gravesides in the gloaming – the 'grimlings' as the Orcadians call the losing struggle of light with dark – and to look around at the chiselled faces, is enough to induce reflections on mortality and history in even the least introspective of people.

Then back for the sandwiches. The Highland Park is liberally dispensed, and the talk is of families. More drams, and the stories start to flow. About Jeanie Flett. Or Thorfin Norquoy. This is living community at work, and as an urban man I am being educated daily, taught about things which are beyond speech. Now, to speak in this way is to move in the direction of romanticism. They smile knowingly at the 'ferryloupers' who come up to Orkney in mid-summer, heading for an island croft they have never even seen, accompanied only by a goat. The simple life is never that simple, as the winter exodus of most of the same people indicates year by year. Islands are not places to escape to. Their basic nature makes you confront yourself, invites you to strip your life down to the essentials, refuses your request to live in a romantic idyll. You must face your darkness if you are to find your life.

The Northern island darkness does things to people. Some go a little crazy. Others compensate by manic optimism. There are fantasists walking around Kirkwall at the moment believing that Scotland are going to beat Brazil heavily in the opening game of the World Cup. I love it.

And some people behave out of character, such as the 500 farmers who demonstrated in the streets of Kirkwall when Donald Dewar came to town last week. Were they victims of Seasonally Affective Disorder? No. They are hardworking people who have been roused to an anger the likes of which this community has not seen for a long time.

FARMERS in Orkney are not normally politicians. They are to be seen on the land, not out in the streets bearing placards. Right now, they feel betrayed.

The difference between Orkney and Shetland has been well described as follows: Shetland consists of fishermen with crofts; Orkney consists of farmers with boats. The rich Orkney farmland has not only been the mainstay of the island economy over centuries, it has helped to feed the country. Its beef has become a byword for quality the world over.

Although there has been very little BSE in Orkney, the European export ban has hit hard.

The farmers here face extraordinarily high transport costs, but the reputation of the product had until now managed to overcome that problem. The farmers felt that the BSE business was covered up politically in the first instance and, when the crisis inevitably exploded, the agricultural community felt itself to be a political football in a posturing European macho tournament in which the goalposts kept moving. What the farmers wanted was a clearly defined way of resolving the crisis – not a single person had any desire to be associated with a product which might cause people harm. The recent 'beef on the bone' statements have further eroded confidence; cattle prices are down, Government subsidies have been cut, and what has made matters worse has been the drop in sheep prices.

The strength of sterling has led to cheap imports from Ireland, setting farmer against farmer. Agricultural income in Orkney has dropped by 28% – a total of £5 million has been wiped out of the Orkney economy this past year.

The Orkney farmers were out in force to 'welcome' Donald Dewar not out of a romantic sense of place, but because they see their community under serious threat. They fear a 1920s style of recession from which the islands may not recover.

The winter darkness goes on. There are days for which 'dreich' is too colourful a term. Yet, even now, there are intimations of a coming glory. Not long now till the shortest day, then the old axis will start to turn again, as it has always done. Springtime and harvest, and the people will be fed again, thanks to the abundance of the dark earth and the work of human hands. The colours will be magical, the light will draw artists and photographers, and stressed-out southerners will appear again with their bemused goats. People will play golf at midnight. The Agricultural Minister will announce a rescue package for the farmers. And, yes, Scotland will beat Brazil.

Nothing wrong with dreaming in the dark is there?

12 December 1997

Blood on our Hands

HE was naked except for a strip of cloth, alone, arms outstretched, a forlorn and abandoned figure. And he was dead, the victim of the fury of an uncontrollable mob. I don't remember his name, but his image is imprinted on my memory.

He was a young man who had hardly learned how to live. He was, as he understood it, only doing his duty. That duty took him to a funeral, to help keep public order. There was a disturbance, then shots, and the crowd of mourners pursued the young man and trampled him to death. Then they went home.

The young British soldier was a victim. Joining up had seemed a better choice than being on the dole. He understood little of the Irish Troubles. He would save up his money, see out his contract, marry, and settle down perhaps, bring up children. It had seemed a good choice at the time. Now he was stretched out, cross-shaped on the green cemetery turf, a Good Friday image, killed in a blood-lust righteous frenzy.

Some years before, bodies of dead and wounded people had lain on the ground. A priest, holding aloft a white handkerchief, was administering the last rites to an unarmed dying young man, slain in an angry hail of bullets. This was a Sunday sacrifice. Bloody Sunday.

It is highly symbolic that the Irish peace process has come to a crux on the brink of the black day we call Good Friday, the day of suffering and abandonment.

There are people who will argue that this conflict has really nothing to do with religion, that it is all a matter of economics and politics. The people who say this are often churchmen, seeking to absolve the Churches of blame for the Troubles. It will not wash, not on Good Friday, nor any other day.

Though the struggle is not just about religion, religious identity is at the heart of it. And behind the struggles in Ireland lie the sins of the Churches, like open wounds. This day, above all days, is not a time for evading truth.

To understand the roots of the Troubles, it is necessary to go back to the Reformation. Many who look at the world through Roman Catholic – and therefore limited – spectacles, will interpret that historical cleavage as the result of pig-headed, self-indulgent rebels putting themselves before the good of the universal Church.

Many who look at the world through Protestant – and therefore limited – lenses will see the reform movement as a glorious time when heroic people stood up for the truth, in the face of a corrupt hierarchy with its corporate hearing-aid switched off.

Many who look at the world through humanist – and therefore limited – prisms, will dismiss all religion as fantastic talk.

It is heartbreaking to read the documents of the time. What is clear is that there was a stage when the looming tragedy could have been averted. What was required on both sides was humility, listening, and faithful action. Some of the great scholars of the Church, such as Erasmus, did their best to mediate. But stubbornness, pride, and power play won the day. Once they were rebuffed, the leaders of the reform movement, instead of sticking it out, walked out of the peace talks and formed their own Churches. Their hierarchical opponents refused to look at any peace plan other than submission.

THUS there were two 'sides', excommunicating each other, producing more and more extreme theological definitions. The Reforming Catholics, on a tide of popular enthusiasm and abetted by political princes who saw advantages in schism, set up alternative Churches. The Roman Catholic Church, in reaction, became much more authoritarian, putting itself out of touching distance of the burgeoning reform movement. The cry, on both sides, was: 'No surrender.'

The rest is poisoned history. The story of Ireland is a particularly extreme acting out of the tragedy, with divided communities telling and retelling only their own versions of history, often full of hatred.

The leaders of the divided communities in Ireland are today being called upon to help each other get out of prison. That requires humility, listening, imagination, and courage. It is very hard for any of us to stand outside of our traditions, adjust our lenses, and dare to see the world in a new way.

Those of us in the Churches are in no position to preach reconciliation while we live division. For the Churches to demand imaginative and courageous action from Irish political leaders and berate them for their failure is simply not on. To applaud deadlines, and encourage Sinn Fein and the Unionists to sit in locked rooms until a solution is found, is one thing. But with the second millennium looming, where are the Church leaders who are prepared to set themselves a similar timetable for a historic and courageous imaginative leap? (This is exactly the process by which the ancient creeds were hammered out.) The Churches need to be freed from their tribal historical prisons as well. Is there an ecclesiastical De Klerk, a Mandela, out there?

Good Friday in Ireland: the passion is set to continue, peace process notwithstanding.

Easter Sunday in Scotland: passion of a different kind. A strangely restless nation, which is increasingly saying 'a plague on all your ecclesiastical houses' – and which would not allow its football team to play later in the day of Diana's funeral – will settle down to watch a football match which the real god, commerce, has dictated will be held on the ancient holy day of resurrection. At the shrine called Ibrox, songs of religious hatred will cascade down from the stands.

As of old, the cry will be 'No Surrender'. Young victims will continue to die, cruciformed. And we in the Churches, with our finery and fine words, custodians of a religion with an inherent capacity for exquisite beauty and transcendent human glory, have blood on our hands.

10 April 1998

Pause
and give
Thanks

IT DOES not seem so long ago since South Africa was heading for a bloodbath. The received wisdom was that blacks, whites, and coloureds were set for an unresolvable conflict which would tear apart that beautiful land. There were few optimists around.

The massacre script was ripped up by two leaders, though many others, through their costly actions and hard work, prepared the way. F W de Klerk, president of South Africa and leader of the white nationalist community, took a courageous and decisive step out of his tribal, defended circle. He knew in his heart that a new future for South Africa could be forged only if he promoted a more inclusive view than the one he had grown up with and which had shaped his political life.

The man who came out of prison, Nelson Mandela, had come to similar conclusions during his long years in Robben Island. Blacks could be truly liberated, he understood, only if the whites were liberated as well.

The word 'miraculous' is over-done, but this awesome exhibition of leadership had transforming power. A friend of ours in South Africa, a Roman Catholic nun, wrote to say how an elderly black woman of her acquaintance bought a new party frock to wear to go to the polls, to vote for the first time in her life.

Another miracle was enacted this week in the city of Belfast. Sworn enemies sat down opposite each other, bolstered by the people's mandate, to work out a new way forward for Northern Ireland.

It's very easy to be cynical and blasé about politics, but what has happened is quite extraordinary. As one who goes regularly on holiday to Ireland, I can testify to the pessimism and despair which has hung over that beautiful land for years. Again, there have been few optimists. At times the Six Counties have hovered on the brink of a horrendous civil war. The notion that David Trimble, Gerry Adams, Ian Paisley, and Martin McGuinness would sit down in the same room, never mind the same parliament, together, seemed like fantasy-thinking. But it has happened. This week. In the flesh.

Before we hurry on with the rest of our lives, we should pause for a few minutes and give thanks. Miracles do happen – not through flashes from the sky or sitting back waiting, but through courage, commitment, hours of black coffee and cigarettes and whisky and tedium, prayer, openness, and sheer humanity.

David Trimble was elected leader of the Ulster Unionists because he was a hardliner. This tough lawyer and unwavering Orangeman was not chosen because he was soft. Let us be clear on how far he has moved. He has embarked on a spiritual and political journey, which could cost him his life, and I don't just mean his political life. He is an extraordinarily brave man, and I salute him.

Let us look at what he said this week: 'We have a historic and honourable opportunity to govern with honour and create a Northern Ireland at peace with itself. I envisage the assembly as a potentially powerful force for creating and strengthening our sense of community and the sense of responsibilities that we have for each other.'

Mr Trimble then went on to make an astonishing statement which shows how he, too, has taken a bold step outside of his tribal, defended circle: 'I want a pluralist parliament for a pluralist people in a Northern Ireland in which all of us, Unionist and nationalist, work together for the benefit of everyone in Northern Ireland.'

WHY is that an astonishing statement? Because the great slogan of Ulster has been: 'A Protestant Parliament for a Protestant People.' A Protestant leader who talks instead about a pluralist parliament for a pluralist people has put himself outside the traditional camp. On face value, to make such a statement is merely to engage in politics for people who do joined-up writing, but in a region reared on partisan slogans this is an extremely dangerous utterance to make. David Trimble is now a man at risk in his own community.

As with Trimble, Gerry Adams is a man I have found difficult to warm to – too much cold steel and calculation. Yet no one should underestimate his courage either. His statements that 'violence must be over, done with, a thing of the past', and that he wishes to be friends with Ian Paisley – that living, bristling, audio-visual aid reminding that tribal religion is part of the problem rather than the solution – now mark Adams as a man at risk as well. There will be frustrated and angry nationalists who will want to get him in their sights – and these particular sights are welded on to very powerful rifles.

For the Ulster gridlock of death to be broken, it required a Unionist leader and a nationalist leader to step outside of their respective laagers. It needed statesmen who were prepared to put themselves on the line. Without that fearless leadership, the peace process was dead in the waters of bitterness.

The roles of John Hume, Mo Mowlam, Bertie Ahern, and Tony Blair should not be underestimated either. The British premier has shown tremendous commitment and political skill to make the Good Friday agreement possible, and he rightly has his place in the history books. (And do not forget the crucial contribution of the haemorrhaging President who is kept alive only by the political life-support system in Washington. That is a measure of the real tragedy of William Jefferson Clinton.)

South Africa's future is still uncertain. So is Northern Ireland's. But this is not the moment to dwell on the huge problems which lie ahead. Think instead of the words uttered this week in Stormont, words which have created a new benchmark for Ireland's future. Spare a thought for the unlikely people who have put their bodies where their mouths are. And if you have prayers, prepare to make them now.

18 September 1998

Alice
and Mary
Stories

A PRIEST working in the east end of Glasgow told me about a cauterising experience he once had. It was an evening mass, and the liturgy that evening required the lighting of a candle at the chapel door, before processing in. As he and the acolyte struggled to light the candle in the breeze, an archetypical wee Glasgow man in a bunnet approached the chapel door and watched the performance with a quizzical look. The Glasgow man – his name is MacLegion – was considerably over-refreshed. Eventually, he summed up the situation pithily in the non-liturgical words: 'Ye'd be as well in yer f......... beds.'

It was the kind of searing judgement that all well-meaning clerics fear, the putative tombstone epitaph that haunts the exhausted dreams. The man with the bunnet could have been the reincarnation of the Old Testament *Qoheleth*, the old cynic who wrote the book of Ecclesiastes – 'Vanity of vanities, all is vanity.'

Today in Glasgow, an outstanding Scotswoman will be buried, and the life of another great Scotswoman will be celebrated. There are lots of people with reason to be grateful that these two got out of their beds every morning. The funeral of Mary More will be held at Maryhill Old Parish Church this morning; and this evening there will be a special service in St Thomas's Church, Gallowgate, honouring the work of Alice Scrimgeour.

Mary who? Alice who? Precisely.

Dr Mary More was a GP who spent 30 years in India with her missionary husband George, one of the wisest and most genuinely radical men I have ever met.

Utterly unpretentious, warm and open, the two of them were greatly loved in the Indian villages in which they lived. Mary was a medical pioneer, providing selfless service without a hint of any Lady Bountiful tendency. When they returned to Scotland, Mary was an unofficial counsellor for many people.

Sixty years ago today, Alice Scrimgeour was commissioned as

a 'Church Sister' in the Church of Scotland. Most of her life-work was in the east end of Glasgow. Everyone who knows Alice loves her – her warmth, her compassion, her humour.

As well as being a practical, down-to-earth woman, Alice has always been a visionary. After the war she took over Stroove, a house in Skelmorlie, and brought youngsters from Germany and Scotland together to talk about, and live, reconciliation.

Stroove became a haven for youngsters and families in the east end of Glasgow who couldn't afford a holiday. The heart of the house was the kitchen. Erik Cramb, for several years minister of St Thomas's, Gallowgate recalls: 'Alice clearly understood that everyone has a tale to tell, but not everyone had someone to listen. In Stroove's basement kitchen, there was a kind of alchemy as youngsters, becoming transfixed by the cooking process, would tell their stories.'

Alice's pancakes are famous. One day, a group of boys from Calton and Drumchapel asked her to make a pancake in the shape of the Scottish Cup. Alice hadn't a clue what it looked like – after all, this Perthshire-born woman was a St Johnstone supporter – but she made what she thought it might

look like. Result – very impressed young men that this old woman knew so much about football.

In that kitchen, people who were often emotionally damaged found themselves affirmed as Alice listened patiently to their tear-strained stories, through endless cups of healing coffee.

Mairi Brown from Calton, when asked by her RE teacher, Jean Young, if she knew any living saints, replied, 'That wummin at Stroove – she must be. She puts up wi' the likes o' us not jist fur wan week but the whole year!'

In the 70s, at the beginning of the Irish troubles, Alice brought kids from both communities for holidays to Strove. One such group included Catholic twins and a Protestant boy. Alice recalled how, on the last day, they said as they skipped along the road arm in arm, 'When we get back to Belfast we'll get together'.

'No,' said one of the twins, 'when we get back to Belfast we'll get shot if we speak to you.'

Alice, typically, has never sought any honours. In 1976, however, the *Evening Times* annual readers' poll for 'Scotswoman of the Year' elected her by a landslide. She was taken to the dinner in the City Chambers in an old clapped-out mini. Alice was diffident about receiving the honour, but when she heard that she was to receive the rosebowl from Frankie Vaughan, she went as weak at the knees as any love-struck teenage devotee. 'He kissed me!' was all people could get out of her after the ceremony.

Alice delights in telling how, in the year that followed, as she did her usual round of speaking to youth fellowships and women's guilds, she was often mis-introduced as 'Miss Scotland' or as 'Sports-woman of the Year'. Bimbo or Liz McColgan she is not.

When she was invited back to the *Evening Times* dinner as a past winner, the Gallowgate congregation, remembering how she had gone to the award in the battered mini, determined that she should go in style this time, in a chauffeur-driven limousine – so they hired the local undertaker to do the honours!

There has never been any dan-ger of Mary More or Alice Scrimgeour being elected Moderator. Yet these two women have totally transcended the indubitably sexist, often patronising assumptions which haunt church structures by their warmth, their humanity, their vision, their humour, and their inclusiveness. They are the kind of people who give Christianity a good name.

Mary and Alice would not have been as well in their beds. These 'east end' women of the world have made a difference to the lives of many people. Neither of them are media celebrities.

Mary More: today, I mourn your passing. Alice Scrimgeour: may this special night, surrounded by friends in the Gallowgate, be a joyous east end celebration of your special and wondrous kitchen theology.

27 March 1998